Ricin!

Ricin!

The Inside Story of the
Terror Plot that Never Was

Lawrence Archer
and
Fiona Bawdon

Foreword by
Michael Mansfield QC

PlutoPress
www.plutobooks.com

First published 2010 by Pluto Press
345 Archway Road, London N6 5AA and
175 Fifth Avenue, New York, NY 10010

www.plutobooks.com

Distributed in the United States of America exclusively by
Palgrave Macmillan, a division of St. Martin's Press LLC,
175 Fifth Avenue, New York, NY 10010

British Library Cataloguing in Publication Data
A catalogue record for this book is available from the British Library

ISBN   978 0 7453 2928 4   Hardback
ISBN   978 0 7453 2927 7   Paperback

Library of Congress Cataloging in Publication Data applied for

This book is printed on paper suitable for recycling and made from
fully managed and sustained forest sources. Logging, pulping and
manufacturing processes are expected to conform to the environmental
standards of the country of origin.

10   9   8   7   6   5   4   3   2   1

Designed and produced for Pluto Press by
Chase Publishing Services Ltd, 33 Livonia Road, Sidmouth, EX10 9JB, England
Typeset from disk by Stanford DTP Services, Northampton, England
Printed and bound in the European Union by
CPI Antony Rowe, Chippenham and Eastbourne

This book is dedicated to the British jury system

Contents

List of Photographs

(between pages 83–92)

1. *Daily Mirror* front page, 8 January 2003.
2. Kamel Bourgass, the only one of the five ricin defendants to be convicted.
3. The shabby flat above a chemist shop in Wood Green, north London, labelled by the media the 'factory of death', following the police raid on 5 January 2003.
4. The exterior of flats in Crumpsall Lane, Manchester.
5. A police officer places flowers outside the Crumpsall Lane property following the tragic death of Stephen Oake.
6. Abu Hamza al-Masri, the firebrand preacher associated with the Finsbury Park Mosque.
7. The Finsbury Park Mosque in north London.
8. Blackstock Road, known as 'Little Algeria'.
9. A Metropolitan Police handout photo, showing AA and other batteries, torch bulbs, superglue, a headset and various other items.
10. Items recovered from the Wood Green raid.
11. Acquitted defendant Mouloud Sihali.

Foreword

Just occasionally you read something which stops you in your tracks. It startles. It reveals. It provokes. This is one such book.

In this age of information overload, of quick-fix sound bites, one event comes fast upon another. Memories fade. Lessons are not learnt. Fact becomes fiction. Myth merges into a mélange of accepted wisdom.

In this instance a myth was perpetrated and perpetuated by the media and by senior UK and US politicians alike. It spread like wildfire, fanning the flames of fear and fuelling the call to arms. The repercussions at all levels – for world peace, democratic accountability and the rule of law – continue to reverberate right through to the present. It concerns a ricin plot that never was. Cutting through this quagmire to restore truth, and its handmaiden justice, from the trappings of prejudice and preconception takes tenacity and fortitude. Above all it requires an independence of mind and spirit to ensure that ordinary common sense prevails. The English Common Law has habitually invoked the apocryphal 'man/woman on the Clapham Omnibus' as a paradigm for these purposes.

In real life we use a jury in the criminal courts to perform this role. A few (12) of our number, representing a randomly selected cross-section of the public, are entrusted to examine the evidence and pass judgement in the form of a verdict. They provide the ultimate protective bastion against arbitrary and overweening governance and they have been doing so for centuries. No surprise, therefore, that their existence has been constantly under threat from successive governments.

Who better, then, to defend this vital civic duty (to bear witness to their essential and enduring integrity) but a voice of conscience from the jury itself.

The pages that follow are a remarkable and extraordinary testament to the fundamental principles of justice. It would have been far easier to remain silent, to walk away at the end of the trial, job done. But conscience would not allow it. The result was a voice of reasoned protest, and an extended hand of friendship and support for men who had been acquitted of terrorism.

Such action by members of a jury is well beyond the call of duty, and so far as I'm aware unprecedented in British legal history. On the other hand English juries have a fine and illustrious tradition of conscientious objection. At the Old Bailey where this trial took place there is a commemorative plaque to another jury. Two Quakers, William Penn and William Mead, were tried in 1670 for sedition and unlawful assembly. Despite increasingly strenuous exhortations by the trial judge the jury refused to convict. They were locked up for two nights, starved and denied tobacco (for some a fate worse than death!). Led by a juror called Bushell they held out and were fined for their intransigence. Four refused to pay the fine and remained in prison for seven months. On appeal they won the right of juries to return verdicts according to their consciences.

This book, however, is not so much about the verdict, because jurors are rightly prohibited from disclosing their deliberations, but more about how their verdict was received and about broader issues raised by the case as a whole. Coincidentally the Chilcot Inquiry has begun to address strikingly similar points, although so far the details of this trial have not surfaced.

There is an array of disturbing questions of public importance which are thrown up by the narrative and which have yet to be answered:

1. Why did the then Prime Minister, Tony Blair, fail to correct his misrepresentations about the existence of 'ricin' in the run up to the Iraq War? (cf. WMD and the September 2002 dossier)

2. How did Colin Powell come to adopt the same misrepresentations before the UN?

3. How is it that Prime Minister Gordon Brown also relied on the same misrepresentations in his arguments about the war on terror?

4. How did highly prejudicial and false stories about gas and poison conspiracies come to be printed in the media?

5. How did the Home Secretary David Blunkett fail to recognise that his adverse comments in a radio interview might compromise a fair trial?

6. On what basis did the Metropolitan Police and the Home Secretary Charles Clarke come to use the ricin case as part of the justification for 90-day detention?

7. To what extent was the source information in the case subject to strict scrutiny in order to exclude any risk of contamination by torture?

8. Why was the jury's verdict subverted by returning the acquitted men to detention in Belmarsh under the SIAC regime?

All these questions have serious implications for the integrity of our political and judicial systems.

For me, however, it is the last question which inflicts the most damage. There is simply no point in engaging a jury to determine one of the most serious charges in the criminal calendar, only for its conclusions to be disregarded. The innuendo at the time, made by both politicians and the media, was largely that the jury got it wrong. So the defendants get locked up again on the same basis as the trial allegation – only this time without trial.

Such a process flagrantly undermines the rule of law and public confidence just as much as the government's decision to go to war in Iraq without a second UN resolution. It is time that the arrogance of such power is severely curbed. It is to be sincerely hoped that the courage of the few will motivate the many.

Michael Mansfield QC
March 2010

Acknowledgements

Lawrence Archer would like to give sincere and heartfelt thanks to the following people:

To my co-writer Fiona Bawdon, for her skill, patience and unswerving commitment to the project.

To my family for their love and loyal support.

To the cleared defendants from the ricin trial, for their time and candid interviews. My particular thanks to Mouloud Sihali and Mustapha Taleb.

To the solicitors, barristers and legal teams who have provided interviews and assistance. In particular Gareth Peirce, Matthew Ryder and Natalia Garcia.

To Michael Mansfield QC for writing the Foreword and his support for this project from its earliest stages.

To the unsung and unassuming members of various voluntary human rights organisations, including Peace and Justice in East London and CAMPACC, for their unstinting help.

To Victoria Brittain, Simon Israel, Livio Zilli, Saleyha Ahsan and Andy Worthington, for their help and invaluable advice.

To some of my fellow jurors, who wish to stay anonymous, for their support.

Lastly to Trudie Burton, for her endless encouragement and belief.

Fiona Bawdon would like to thank the following people:

My family – Tim, Caleb and Saul – for everything, always.

Lawrence Archer, for putting his head above the parapet (and keeping it there).

Robert Brown and Gemma Tombs at Corker Binning for their expertise, generously and speedily given.

Wesley Gryk for his advice and help with Chapter 3.

Introduction

One Sunday morning, almost exactly a year after the end of the ricin trial, three former jurors are standing outside Old Street Tube station in central London. None of them has ever done anything like this before, and they are feeling distinctly sheepish. A couple of them are smoking nervously as they discuss what to expect; it feels like waiting for a blind date, only a thousand times more nerve-wracking.

The trio were thrown together by the British legal system. They are ordinary people, doing ordinary jobs, who were picked at random in 2004 to sit on the jury for one of the most significant and high-profile terrorism cases the UK has ever seen. On the face of it, they are unlikely candidates to be making legal history. The former jury foreman (and co-author of this book), Lawrence Archer, is a 51-year-old telephone engineer, who has worked at the same company for 16 years. He drives a five-year-old Ford and lives in an outer London suburb with his wife and two children. His fellow jurors are also Londoners: a 31-year-old product manager and a 30-year-old civil servant.

What they are about to do on this morning, however, is extraordinary – probably unprecedented in the history of British criminal justice. After months of discussing and agonising among themselves, they are about to meet two of the defendants in the trial. They have already met one of the other defendants, when they went along to Mustapha Taleb's asylum hearing a few weeks earlier.

These three Algerians – along with two other defendants – were accused of taking part in a sophisticated terrorist plot to unleash deadly poison on the UK public. One defendant, Kamel Bourgass, was convicted of conspiracy, the other four were acquitted of all charges. Despite being found not guilty, the government is attempting to deport them on the grounds that they are a threat to national security, relying in large part on evidence which was discredited at the ricin trial.

To add to the sense of unreality as the jurors wait, a black-clad Goth and his similarly attired girlfriend begin a loud argument across the street, which rapidly degenerates into a scuffle. The man comes off worse, mainly because the woman, who is wearing huge boots, repeatedly kicks him in the groin. Eventually, he skulks off in the other direction and relative peace is restored.

Suddenly, there's a man in a baseball cap and casual clothes walking towards them, grinning from ear to ear. The three jurors sat just metres away from him almost everyday for six months and they know more about him and his life than they do about many members of their own family, yet they barely recognise the smiling and relaxed figure sauntering in their direction as David Khalef.

Khalef always wore a jacket and tie in court, but another reason he looks different today is that he is wearing a brightly coloured mobile phone strap around his neck, bearing the words 'Sexy Chick'. His English has improved since his days in court (when every word had to be translated for him by an interpreter), but it seems there is still some way to go...

Khalef greets the three jurors with hugs and, to the great embarrassment of the foreman's English sensibilities, kisses on both cheeks. He seems remarkably at ease and is clearly very pleased to see them.

Mouloud Sihali appears soon after, walking with a heavy limp. He also greets the jurors warmly but, to the foreman's great relief, there are no kisses this time. He is clearly intelligent and has excellent English. There is a seriousness about him and he insists on paying for everyone's coffee, even though at this point he is living on benefits of around £40 a week. Later, he is obviously highly embarrassed when the jurors insist on paying for lunch and orders the cheapest thing on the menu.

Sihali is still deeply affected by his experiences – not least physically. The limp is a legacy of the force used by police when he was re-arrested a few weeks after the July 2005 attacks on London commuters, and his general health is fragile.

For Sihali, talking to the people who had decided his fate a year earlier at the ricin trial seems to be like a dam being breached. Over lunch, a torrent of information pours out of him, as if his life depended on telling the jurors everything he can about himself, the supposed plot, and what has happened to him since. Sihali is such a mine of facts and figures that Archer (who later nicknames him 'Encyclopaedia Ricinica') begins to take copious notes, which will ultimately form the basis for this book.

Over the following months and years, Lawrence Archer will continue to follow the lives of the former defendants and will develop a particularly warm and genuine friendship with Mouloud Sihali. Archer will spend many hours talking to the four about their lives here and in Algeria, and how they came to be mixed up with Bourgass and his fellow plotter Mohammed Meguerba.

The resulting book tells the full story of the trial for the first time. The legacy of the so-called 'Wood Green ricin plot' is far-reaching. It was offered as evidence by both the British and American governments to bolster the case for war on Iraq, and was later cited by UK politicians to argue for Draconian anti-terror measures, including the introduction of ID cards. Yet these arguments are built on sand, based on a case riddled with misinformation that involved serious mistakes and incompetence by the authorities, including the suppression for many weeks of the fact that no ricin had been found during police raids. The case had other dubious ramifications, not least that it served to re-establish friendly political relations between the UK and Algeria, a country previously widely ostracised for its appalling human rights record and use of torture in interrogations.

Rarely has a legal case been so shamelessly co-opted by ministers, the media and the security forces to reinforce their own agendas. At times, they fed off each other, until all sense of truth or reality was lost. Yet beyond the screaming headlines and tub-thumping political rhetoric, there are the untold human stories of those caught up in the trial. This book gives a rare insight into the lives of the asylum seekers, living below the radar, who were sucked into the maelstrom of the ricin plot; it is also the story of a small group of jurors, ordinary people, who decided that ultimately, sometimes, you have to make a stand.

1
The Trial

On 8 April 2005, after 17 days of deliberation following a six-month trial, the jurors filed back into court 16 at the Old Bailey.

The press box was filled with journalists waiting to hear the verdicts in what had been the first major UK terror trial since the 9/11 attacks on America. The so-called 'ricin plot trial' had been an unprecedented case, with defence lawyers predicting the five men would face up to 30 years in prison if convicted.

The jury foreman, Lawrence Archer, stood. One by one the verdicts were read out.

Mouloud Sihali? Not guilty on all charges.

David Khalef? Not guilty on all charges.

Sidali Feddag? Not guilty on all charges

Mustapha Taleb? Not guilty on all charges.

The fifth defendant was Kamel Bourgass, the alleged ringleader of the plot. In his case, the jury found him guilty of conspiracy to cause a 'public nuisance' by using explosives or poisons to spread fear or disruption. As far as the more serious charge of conspiracy to murder was concerned, the jurors remained deadlocked. (After two further days of inconclusive deliberation, the jury was dismissed by the judge on 12 April 2005.)

The string of acquittals, and a single conviction on the lesser (albeit still serious) charge was not at all the result the government had expected when the ricin trial opened in September 2004. It certainly wasn't much to show for a trial costing an estimated £20 million, which ran for seven months and where the prosecution evidence alone took four months to put before the jury.

The trial that began on 13 September 2004 was the result of a series of dramatic police raids between September 2002 and January 2003. The resulting newspaper headlines were alarming in the extreme: the police had uncovered an active and deadly 'poison factory' and succeeded in breaking up a network of determined Al-Qaeda terrorists. The *Sun*: 'Ricin near Bin pal's home' ('The poison factory used to make deadly ricin is just 200 yards from the lair of one of Osama bin Laden's henchmen...').[1] *Daily Mail*: 'Ricin assassin on the run' ('Police were last night hunting a lone assassin who slipped through their dragnet as they swooped on a London-based terrorist cell manufacturing the poison ricin...').[2]

The usually more temperate media took an equally alarmist line. The BBC reported that gas-mask sales had 'soared' following the ricin find. The manager of an army surplus shop was quoted as saying: 'My niece lives in London and she and her husband took gas masks down there. People are worried about the tube.'[3]

Two days later, the BBC claimed the FBI had been put on alert for ricin. Agents were warned that the toxin would be 'most effective in an assassination by injection or as a food contaminant', but could also be used 'to contaminate closed ventilation systems, water supplies, lakes and rivers'.[4]

The *Independent* newspaper also stressed that the plot was part of an international conspiracy. The finds in north London were being linked to a Europe-wide 'network of terrorist assassination squads', intent on carrying out 'random killings using exotic poison ... designed to maximise panic and fear'.[5]

When the trial opened at the Old Bailey 18 months later, five Algerian men were in the dock. Kamel Bourgass, Mouloud Sihali, David Khalef, Sidali Feddag and Mustapha Taleb stood accused of a terrorist plot, involving homemade explosives and poisons, including the deadly toxin ricin.

A further trial of four other defendants, all facing similar charges and with links to the alleged ricin plotters in the initial trial, was planned to follow on directly afterwards. However, even before it started, the trial must have been something of a let down for those who saw the arrests as vindicating the government's tough anti-terror stance. For all the lurid newspaper headlines at the time of their arrests, earlier charges of manufacturing a chemical weapon had been dropped in the run up to the trial.

Bourgass was said to be the leader of the terror cell along with another man, Mohammed Meguerba, who, although absent from the Old Bailey dock, was to have a central role in the proceedings.

The spectre of Meguerba, an Algerian in his mid-thirties, haunted the trial. In the summer of 2002, Meguerba had been an associate of Bourgass's in London but fled the UK later that year after being questioned and then released by anti-terror police. By December 2002, he was back in Algeria. What the ricin jurors weren't told was that, on his return, Meguerba had been interrogated and almost certainly tortured by the notorious Algerian secret service – and it was this evidence that alerted British security forces to the ricin plot and led to the arrests of Bourgass and the other defendants. This information about Meguerba was only one of several key facts which were kept from the jurors in the interests of ensuring a fair trial and which only emerged after they had delivered their verdicts.

Sitting in the glass-walled box of the prisoners' dock at the Old Bailey, Bourgass made for an unlikely terror suspect: with his meek manner and wire-rimmed glasses, he looked more like a librarian than a master terrorist. However, Bourgass – who went under a variety of names, including Nadir Habra and Omar Rami – was alleged to be the ringleader and main organiser of the plot. The prosecution claimed the poison recipes seized by police were in his handwriting and that his fingerprints were all over the ingredients and equipment allegedly stockpiled for making poisons and explosives which had been seized during the raids.

Entirely unbeknown to the jurors throughout the ricin trial, Bourgass was already the convicted killer of a police officer. In June 2004, Bourgass had been found guilty at the Old Bailey and sentenced to life imprisonment for the fatal stabbing of Detective Constable Stephen Oake during his arrest in Manchester. Three other police officers were also injured in what was a frenzied attack. However, Bourgass's convictions for murder and wounding had not been reported in the media so as to avoid prejudicing the subsequent ricin trial – and the jury only learned about them once the trial had ended.

Bourgass's co-defendants were accused of having lesser but still significant roles in the ricin plot. They were a ragbag bunch for the jury to look at, ranging from the pimply teenager Sidali Feddag, to the thuggish-looking Mustapha Taleb.

The most striking of the four was Mouloud Sihali. Tall, good-looking, and well educated with fluent English, Sihali was accused of having a pivotal role as a general 'Mr Fix-it', supplying the plotters with finance and false documents, as well as a safe house for Meguerba before he had skipped the country.

Sihali often shared a room with another defendant, David Khalef, but the pair appeared to have little in common. Whereas Sihali was urbane and clearly intelligent, Khalef was largely illiterate with a low IQ. Khalef spoke little English and relied on an interpreter throughout the trial. He was accused by the prosecution of providing safekeeping for one of the poison recipes that Bourgass had written out.

The youngest defendant was Sidali Feddag, just 17 when he was arrested and still sporting teenage acne at the time of the trial. It was alleged that he had let the lead conspirator, Bourgass, stay in his bed-sit in north London.

The final defendant was Mustapha Taleb, who had a habit of staring straight at the jurors. With his hard-faced and shaven-headed appearance, he could easily have been mistaken for the leader of the plot but, in fact, was alleged to be a minor player, accused of photocopying the poison recipes in the bookshop at Finsbury Park Mosque where he worked.

The five defendants each faced two counts: conspiracy to murder; and conspiracy to cause a public nuisance. One defendant, Mouloud Sihali, also faced a further five charges of possessing false or doctored passports.

There was an awful lot riding on the trial – and not just for the defendants who potentially faced lengthy jail terms. It was a trophy trial for the authorities: convictions would give a huge boost to the government, police and security services in their efforts to show the UK was winning the so-called 'war on terror'. A successful prosecution would help allay public fears and bolster support for controversial anti-terror laws which had recently been introduced.

The judge presiding over the historic trial was Mr Justice David Penry-Davey. Penry-Davey, aged 60 at the time, was appointed a high court judge in 1997 and is well liked and respected at the Bar. He is not a typical judge. A towering figure, standing 6 foot 7 inches tall, Penry-Davey is a product of Hastings Grammar School and King's College London, rather than having taken the more traditional route to the judiciary of public school and Oxbridge. Even less typically, the year before the ricin trial, Penry-Davey made newspaper headlines as a 'have-a-go hero' when he tackled a gang of seven muggers who attacked him at a train station. Despite being punched and kicked to the ground, the judge ran after the muggers, commandeered the car of a passing motorist and managed to retrieve most of his stolen property.

Penry-Davey was also a self-proclaimed believer in the wisdom of juries. In 1996, he told the *Independent*: 'You shouldn't see it as a failure if someone is acquitted. ... My experience over many years tells me that generally, [juries] have got it right.'[6]

Opening the case for the prosecution was Nigel Sweeney QC, a highly experienced prosecutor, who had appeared in numerous other terrorist cases, including the trial of those accused of the 1984 IRA bombing of the then Conservative government at the Grand Hotel in Brighton. It took Sweeney three days just to outline the prosecution case against the five men in the ricin case, such was the detail and complexity of the accusations. He told the jury that all the defendants were involved to some degree or another in a plot to make and use poisons and/or explosives.

Sweeney opened with a dramatic description of the 5 January 2003 police raid on a flat at 352b High Road, Wood Green. Wood Green is an insalubrious area of north London popular among Algerians and other immigrants because of the availability of cheap rental accommodation. A room in the flat at 352b had been leased to the teenager Sidali Feddag since September 2001, but by summer 2002 it was regularly used as a place to stay by Bourgass who had nowhere permanent to live.

Sweeney told the jury that the police raid on 5 January uncovered a treasure trove of apparently incriminating items. Police found a locked sports bag belonging to Bourgass, containing £4,100 in cash and, of far more interest to the authorities, a lengthy document in Arabic. The document in Bourgass's handwriting turned out to be a series of recipes for poison and explosives. It described the ingredients and manufacturing processes for various toxins, including cyanide, nicotine and ricin, and instructions for making explosives similar to those that were used two years later in the 7/7 London bombings. There was also a diagram of a detonator and a separate list of chemicals, showing their usual household names, common uses and where they could be obtained.

Sweeney then took the jury through Feddag's arrest and the evidence the teenager had subsequently given to police at Paddington Green police station.

Feddag had come to England from Algeria in 2000 with his father. The older man had subsequently returned to his home country, leaving his 15-year-old son in the care of a family friend in east London. The boy had applied for asylum but he failed to turn up for an immigration interview and remained in the country illegally.

His illegal immigration status did not, however, prevent Feddag from receiving help with housing. In September 2001, Islington Council Asylum Team had found him the room at 352b High Road, Wood Green – the address the media were later to describe as a 'factory of death'.[7]

Feddag lived at Wood Green, surviving hand to mouth, for about a year. But, in the summer of 2002, he moved back to east London to house-sit for the family friend, who had had to return to Algeria following the death of his mother.

A spare room was a precious commodity among the Algerian community, so rather than leave 352b standing empty, Feddag had offered it to Bourgass, whom he knew as 'Nadir'. The two knew each other slightly via the Finsbury Park Mosque and Feddag was aware that Nadir didn't have a permanent place to live.

The prosecution barrister, Nigel Sweeney, reeled off a list of items found at the Wood Green premises which he said were for use in the making of poisons or explosives: rubber gloves, scales, thermometers, blotting paper, a funnel, three plastic bottles of acetone (the principal ingredient in nail varnish remover) and isopropanol (rubbing alcohol), a coffee mill, a mortar and pestle, fruit seeds and a total of 22 castor beans, most of which were kept, incongruously, in a pink jewellery box.

Evidence from the police officer who interviewed Feddag after the 17-year-old's arrest was read to the court. Feddag had insisted throughout these interviews that all the suspect items belonged to Bourgass, the man he knew as Nadir. Feddag seemed to think that the items were entirely innocent and didn't apparently question why Bourgass had wanted to stockpile such a curious array of goods. Feddag's claim that all these belonged to Bourgass was supported by the fact that none of Feddag's fingerprints had been found on any of the items – whereas Bourgass's prints were all over them.

The officer testified that Feddag had been generally helpful during questioning – answering everything he was asked and going through a large number of photographs to identify various people he knew, mainly from the Finsbury Park Mosque.

The Finsbury Park Mosque in north London is best known for being a centre for radical Islam. However, even at the height of its notoriety, the mosque's role was much wider than that, acting as a magnet for many young Algerian men, who used it as a social as well as religious centre.

During questioning, Feddag had confessed to police to holding a false passport in the fictitious name of Osman Koufi, and to having tried to buy one for his brother, who was due to arrive in London from Algeria. At the end of 2002, Feddag had asked Bourgass to vacate the room at 352b, so his brother could stay there instead and, as a result, Bourgass was no longer living at the flat when the police raided.

The prosecution barrister then turned to the recipes in Bourgass's handwriting that had been found at Feddag's flat. On the pieces of paper found by police, Bourgass had written out instructions for producing five different poisons in total: cyanide, botulinum (which he called 'rotten meat poison'), nicotine poison ('cigarette poison'), solanine ('potato poison') and ricin ('castor bean poison'). He had also noted an indication of the deadliness of each of the toxins ('X milligrams of poison will result in X number of deaths'), with one estimating that 80,000 people could die from a single dose.

The prosecution called on an expert in toxicology and biological warfare from the government laboratory at Porton

Down who testified that the figures quoted by Bourgass were largely accurate: the poisons listed were potentially extremely dangerous and deadly. In the words of the prosecution barrister, they were 'no playtime recipes'.

The public gallery was screened off during the toxicology expert's evidence and he was referred to throughout only as 'Dr A'. Although these measures added to the already heightened atmosphere in the court, the doctor's identity was being concealed not because of safety concerns arising from the ricin trial but to protect him from the threat of attacks from animal rights activists who object to the Porton Down laboratory's use of animal testing.

Dr A explained that scientists at Porton Down had followed the instructions as written in the Bourgass recipes, to see what they produced. Dr A went through his team's findings in turn.

The ingredients listed for producing cyanide included fruit seeds, such as apple pips and cherry stones. Dr A testified that it would be possible to make cyanide following Bourgass's recipe – but not with the tiny amounts of seeds that had been found at the flat. Sack-loads of fruit would be needed to make a single lethal dose, making it a highly inefficient and unlikely method of production, he said. Dr A added that there are far more efficient ways for a determined poisoner to make cyanide, such as by simply combining the relevant chemicals.

Bourgass's recipe for homemade botulinum – the bacteria which causes botulism poisoning – was even more unlikely. It detailed making a dough from ground corn and water, adding rotten meat and dung, covering the concoction with water and keeping it warm in a sealed flask for a few days. Dr A explained the theory behind the recipe: the dung was to provide the initial source of botulinum bacteria; the dough provided food for the bacteria to grow; and the airtight flask would create the conditions where the bacteria could flourish. However, while the theory might be sound, the practice was decidedly hit and miss, he explained: there was no way of knowing whether a particular dung sample actually contained botulinum bacteria, and it would be difficult to ensure the perfect seal on the flask needed to create the optimum conditions for the bacteria to grow.

Dr A confirmed that, while the recipe would produce a very nasty concoction – anyone swallowing it would certainly be extremely sick – it was unlikely to produce the desired deadly botulinum.

Among the items found by police in Feddag's flat was a sludgy brown liquid in a Nivea face-cream pot which, on analysis, was found to be a mixture of nicotine, isopropanol and water. Although smokers routinely inhale small amounts of nicotine, Dr A explained that nicotine could kill if a large enough dose was injected. However, whether this brown substance was Bourgass's crude attempt to make 'nicotine poison' was not explored during questioning.

The third toxin on Bourgass's list was solanine, which is made from the shoots and green parts of the potato plant. Dr A explained that, depending on the dose, its effects range from diarrhoea and vomiting, to fever, paralysis and even death. He described the method for extracting solanine in the recipes as crude and said that the amount produced from the quantity of potatoes suggested was unlikely to be fatal.

Finally, Dr A turned to the subject of ricin – the apparent discovery of which had generated alarming headlines at the time of the police raid. The scientist described how he had analysed some of the 22 castor beans found at the Wood Green flat and they had, indeed, contained natural ricin. Although ricin is difficult to produce outside of laboratory conditions, he concluded that the method used in the handwritten recipes to extract the poison was crude but essentially workable, although the tiny amount of ricin produced would be enough for only one dose.

The recipes had suggested the ricin would be produced as a fine powder at the end of the process. Dr A said he was surprised that, although the instructions advised using gloves, there was no mention of wearing a protective mask, as the powder could easily be inhaled during manufacture. No masks were found at the Wood Green flat, although the prosecution suggested the plotters could have tied a cloth over the mouth and nose as an improvised mask.

From Dr A's measured evidence, it seemed that, however malevolent Bourgass's intentions, the defendant's DIY attempts at poison-making were amateurish in the extreme – more Fred Karno than Al-Qaeda. The reality of what the police had found in the so-called 'factory of death' was nowhere near as dramatic or deadly as press reports at the time of the raids had apparently suggested. However, a further surprise was in store about the prosecution case.

Dr A had been one of the first people into the Wood Green flat after the police, with the task of trying to identify anything potentially poisonous. At this stage, he had conducted an initial 'presumptive' test on various items which could have been used in the manufacture of poisons. The presumptive test is a generic marker for proteins, used to indicate whether there is anything that might cause concern and should be subjected to more definitive analysis.

Most of the items Dr A tested showed negative, but results for the pestle and mortar were potentially more interesting to the police. They showed a 'very weak positive reaction' which could have meant ricin – but was not at all definitive.

Dr A would need to conduct further, more sophisticated tests back at Porton Down to find out for sure.

Once back in his laboratory at Porton Down, the doctor had used the far more specific Elisa test on the pestle and mortar. This time, the result had come back negative: no ricin. At the behest of his superiors, he subsequently conducted another test, this time based on DNA profiling – although Dr A himself was sceptical of the value of this kind of test, as he believed it was too new and untried to be worthwhile. When the results from the DNA test came back, they too were inconclusive. Overall, the scientist told the court, he was not convinced there were any traces of ricin on the pestle and mortar, after all.

In other words, no ricin. Indeed, no poison of any kind had been discovered in the raid on the Wood Green flat – a fact which had been known within two days of the raid on 5 January.

The startling admission that the 'ricin plot' had not actually involved the discovery of any ricin brought Bourgass's defence barrister, Michel Massih QC, to his feet. Massih waved a copy of the *Daily Mirror* newspaper dated 8 January 2003 around the court. The *Daily Mirror*'s front page could hardly have been more alarming or more unequivocal. Under the words 'Deadly terror poison found in Britain' was the huge headline: 'IT'S HERE'.[8] The rest of the page was taken up with a map of Britain covered by a black skull and crossbones. Inside, coverage of the raid on the supposed 'terror lab' ran to six pages; hospitals were 'on doomsday watch', it warned, on alert for people already suffering signs of ricin poisoning.

Why, Michel Massih wanted to know, was the media printing alarming reports about a so-called ricin plot when it had already been established that no ricin had ever actually been found?

Dr A said it was not a question he could answer – but it was one which was soon to be put to the next witness to give evidence, Andrew Gould.

Andrew Gould was a colleague of Dr A's at Porton Down. He was a manager, rather than a scientist, and it was his job to pass on the test findings to the anti-terror police at SO13 who were working on the case.

Could Gould explain how the idea of a 'ricin plot' had taken hold? Gould admitted under questioning that he had, indeed, told police that ricin had been positively detected at the flat – despite the lack of any definitive test results. His admission was met with disbelief by Bourgass's barrister. Why had Gould told the police ricin had been found when the test results didn't back this up? Gould's explanation, which he stuck to despite fierce questioning from Massih, was that he had done so as a protective measure because of safety concerns following the initial 'weak positive' result. He had, he said, told police ricin had been found – even though the initial result was equivocal – so they would proceed with appropriate caution in their search of the premises. It was the information that Gould had passed to the police which ended up in the media and led to banner headlines about the ricin plot.

Gould was then pressed by the defence on why, even when the more definitive negative test results came back two days after the raid, he had not corrected the wrong information previously given to police. His response was that it 'was not his job to get involved in politics'. In fact, Porton Down did not inform police or ministers of the true position until March – a delay of three months – by which time the myth of the 'ricin plot' had firmly taken root in the imagination of the media and the public.

Gould's evidence that no ricin had been positively identified showed that the ricin-plot hare had been set running by a false positive test result and a decision taken by a non-scientist employee at Porton Down. What's more, no one had sought to calm public fears by correcting the wrong information which had been given to police until three months later, despite the raft of alarming and inaccurate press stories the false reports of a ricin find had generated.

The next barrister to cross-examine Gould was Michael Mansfield QC, who was acting for Mouloud Sihali, the man described by the prosecution as the plot's Mr Fix-it.

Michael Mansfield is the closest thing the barristers' profession has to a household name. He has a long pedigree in heavy-duty criminal defence work, although is better known in recent years for appearing at the inquests into the deaths of Princess Diana and the Stockwell shooting victim, Jean Charles de Menezes. Mansfield has a well-earned reputation for taking difficult and unpopular cases and for being a tough cross-examiner, as Gould was about to find out.

Mansfield began gently enough, asking Gould about his work at Porton Down. The barrister seemed particularly interested in the procedures for note keeping, and Gould went into considerable detail about where he would have kept his notes of the crucial test findings that had been relayed to him by his scientist colleagues. Given the sensitivity of the results, Gould explained that his notes would have been kept in a locked filing cabinet, to which only he and another colleague had access.

Initially, it seemed an innocuous line of questioning, certainly compared with Massih's full frontal assault. However, as

Mansfield continued to press Gould, it was clear that the barrister attached great significance to these notes. Why, asked Mansfield, had Gould not retrieved his notes from the filing cabinet where they were stored to refresh his memory when subsequently making his statement to the police? Isn't it terribly difficult, Mansfield asked, to remember events of 18 months earlier without some kind of aide memoire?

At this point, Gould appeared to falter. Mansfield pressed on: why hadn't he referred to the notes that he had previously taken and carefully stored? The exchange went on for several minutes as Gould attempted to explain why he had not drawn on these crucial records for his police statement. Finally, after a direct challenge from Mansfield, Gould made a surprise admission: contrary to his earlier assertions, he had not taken any notes of the various test findings as a result of the Wood Green raid; the reason he hadn't referred to notes when making his police statement was because they didn't exist.

The admission was met with stunned silence. Gould had misled the court and was now obliged to correct his previous evidence to clarify that he had not made any notes of the various test results; he wished he had, but he hadn't.

Mansfield's demolition of Gould was a moment of real drama in the trial, like something out of a Hollywood film. However, although film-makers love to use witness-box confessions as a dramatic device, in reality it is rare for new or surprising information to emerge during cross-examination. Of itself, the fact Gould hadn't kept notes was a fairly small point – but misleading the court about it was a different matter. Gould – who had done so much to create the myth of the ricin plot – exited the witness box soon after.

After Gould's departure, the court heard from an array of experts, each giving evidence on different technical aspects of the case.

First up was an explosives expert who confirmed that Bourgass's handwritten recipes were capable of producing a bomb. The recipes had mentioned various types of explosive, most of which could be manufactured from domestic products or easily obtainable chemicals. These included a 'fertilizer bomb', made from ammonium nitrate, a form of explosives previously used to devastating effect by the Irish Republican terror group, the IRA.

Most of the explosives mentioned in the recipes were high explosives – having a fast burn rate and capable of causing extensive damage. They were designed to be packed into a sealed container to allow pressure to build up and blow apart, producing shrapnel to maximise injuries. Most of them could create a bigger explosion if combined with petrol or some other accelerant.

The jury was told that the explosives would need a detonator – a smaller explosive device to trigger the main blast – which would normally be fired electrically. Although all the recipes were capable of making a bomb, some would be highly unstable and deteriorate rapidly after being manufactured and so were unlikely to be made by a novice bomb-maker.

Next into the witness box was an electronics expert, who also testified to the potentially deadly nature of Bourgass's writings and drawings. She had studied the detonator diagram which was also shown on the recipes and, with minor modifications, had been able to build a working detonator, which she brought along to court in a pizza box. The detonator mock-up made beeping sounds every now and then to show that the circuit was indeed working.

Bourgass's recipes were not the kind of thing an average, peaceable citizen would have in his possession. But what was yet to be established was whether there was ever any real intention to act on the information – given that no explosives or bomb-making ingredients were recovered from any of the premises searched in connection with the trial.

One possible clue to Bourgass's intentions was given by the next witness, a handwriting expert. The expert testified that the recipes were in the same handwriting as a prayer found at Wood Green that Bourgass admitted he had written. However, the expert added that, not only had Bourgass written out the recipes in the first place, he had amended them later on, by adding extra details.

In fact, the police had found four copies of the recipes during the course of their investigations – three at the Wood Green flat, plus another at the Thetford home of Bourgass's fellow defendant David Khalef. The original was the recipe that Bourgass had left in the sports bag, along with £4,100 in cash, at Wood Green. Two of the three other versions were photocopies of the original, which the expert testified had been altered by Bourgass, who had made various amendments in a different coloured pen. There was also a third smaller handwritten version. The prosecution claimed that the changes to the photocopies showed that Bourgass hadn't just written out the recipes for his own amusement, but that he had been refining them, suggesting that he'd had every intention of using them at some stage.

One day of the handwriting expert's evidence was marked by the appearance in court of the vast photocopying machine that police had seized from the Finsbury Park Mosque. The expert explained that the version of the recipes which police had found in Thetford had been made on the mosque photocopier. The Thetford photocopy had, in turn, been copied (this time by a machine at a shop in Ilford) and this version was the one that had been found at the bottom of the wardrobe in Wood Green.

Another item found at Wood Green was a set of electronic scales, which could measure small weights extremely accurately. On the instructions for these scales, somebody had written a set of calculations which appeared to match the ratio of castor beans to acetone cited in the recipe for producing ricin. The expert testified that, although the handwriting looked very much like Bourgass's, this couldn't be proved conclusively. However, it seemed that someone – whether Bourgass or another person – had actually attempted to work out how to make a small batch of the poison.

A key plank of the prosecution case was fingerprint evidence which they claimed showed connections between the defendants and that they had handled incriminating material.

The fingerprint expert, Kirsty Ball, went into painstaking detail about whose prints had been found where – but, of course, it was up to the jury to decide what the significance of these finds might be.

Bourgass's fingerprints had been found all over the recipes and the equipment which the prosecution alleged were for making poisons, so there was no doubt that he had repeatedly handled these items.

A fingerprint belonging to Mustapha Taleb, the defendant with the thuggish appearance, had been found on the back of one set of the poison recipes. Clearly, Taleb had handled at least one of the recipes. However, Taleb's barrister, Ben Emmerson QC, was to argue that the position of the prints was consistent with Taleb's simply having put the document face down on a photocopier during the course of his work at the mosque. There was nothing to show he had ever looked at the content of the recipes. Apart from these inconclusive fingerprints, there was nothing to link Taleb with the Wood Green 'poisons factory' at all.

There were no prints from the teenager Sidali Feddag on any of the recipes or the suspect items found at the flat. Similarly, there was no fingerprint evidence to link the smartly dressed Mouloud Sihali with the recipes or poison-making equipment. However, Sihali's prints had been detected on an envelope containing stolen and altered passports, which had been found in a bed base at 240 High Road, Ilford, the property he shared with David Khalef.

David Khalef's prints had been found on the set of recipes found in his bag at Thetford, but not on any of the Wood Green items.

Kirsty Ball also testified that fingerprints belonging to Mohammed Meguerba, Bourgass's associate who had fled to Algeria after being questioned by police, had been found on the poison recipes.

There was evidence linking both Bourgass and the absent Meguerba to the alleged poisoning plot, but the involvement of the other defendants had yet to be explored.

The prosecution's conspiracy case depended on proving links between the five men. At one point, to try to show them the complex web of connections, the jurors were handed a bundle of papers, which gave each defendant a colour code and listed the various telephone contacts between them.

By now the trial, which had started in September, had been running for three months. It was clear the judge's earlier prediction that it would be finished by end of January was hopelessly optimistic. Ramadan came and went and, with

Christmas looming, still the jurors had not heard from any of the five defendants in the witness box.

After a longer-than-expected Christmas break (the re-start of the trial was delayed because of legal argument between the prosecution and defence), the jurors returned to the Old Bailey to find the case had been moved from Court 8 to Court 16, which had a bigger dock with a higher protective glass screen.

Security in the new court was stepped up: extra officers were stationed in the dock with the defendants and armed police were posted at various points around the court, including two in the public gallery. Officers with guns were also stationed all around the streets outside the court and in overlooking buildings; and a helicopter started accompanying the defendants on their journeys to and from the court. No explanation was given for the heightened security.

Finally, in January 2005, after nearly four months of evidence, the prosecution announced it had finished setting out its case.

There had been no dramatic conclusion to the Crown case against the defendants. Barrister Nigel Sweeney had built his conspiracy case largely on the evidence of expert witnesses and the loose alleged connections between the defendants. There had been no witnesses of fact, to testify to having seen or heard the defendants do anything suspicious. After so many weeks, Sweeney had not produced any single piece of damning evidence. Instead, he had left many conclusions dangling, unspoken, in the hope the jury would knit them together to make a conspiracy.

Now it was the turn of the defence. If the prosecution case had ended more with a whimper than a bang, the defence seemed about to get off to a dramatic start. When the defence

began its case on 19 January, the first witness to be called was
the figure at the centre of the alleged plot, Kamel Bourgass.

Bourgass didn't look much like anyone's idea of a terrorist
mastermind. Slight and wiry, he was dwarfed by the security
guards who escorted him from the dock to the witness box.
He was in his early thirties, had short woolly black hair, a
neatly trimmed moustache and wire-rimmed glasses, which all
combined to give him the air of a meek-mannered librarian.

Whereas his fellow defendants Mouloud Sihali and David
Khalef had always been smartly dressed in court, wearing a
jacket and tie on most days, Bourgass always wore a grey
sports sweatshirt. His clothes hung baggily, giving him the
appearance of a small boy wearing hand-me-downs.

The first surprise was when the defendant, speaking
through an interpreter, announced that his name was not, in
fact, Kamel Bourgass, but Nadir Habra – and this was the
name he used throughout the rest of the trial (although we
will refer to him here as Kamel Bourgass to avoid confusion).

Via the interpreter, his barrister, Michel Massih, started by
asking Bourgass about his past, his family and his upbringing.
Massih then moved on to ask about the recipes. Although
Bourgass had admitted they were in his handwriting, he
insisted they weren't really anything to do with him: he had
simply written them out at the request of his former associate
Mohammed Meguerba (who was, of course, by that stage
being held in Algeria).

Bourgass claimed that Meguerba had no intention of using
the recipes to attack UK citizens. Instead, he wanted them to
help defend villagers back in his native Algeria. According to
Bourgass, Meguerba wanted to give the recipes to villagers in
the Setif region so they could fight back against raids by the
government militia, who would brazenly seize food, money

and goods, often killing anyone who resisted. Meguerba's plan was to help the villagers get revenge on their attackers by poisoning any food supplies that might be stolen. Meguerba had asked Bourgass to write the recipes out for him because he thought the latter 'had neat handwriting'.

Bourgass's unexpected change of name (to Nadir Habra) had initially wrong-footed his own barrister (who stumbled over the new name a few times) and the fact that Bourgass had failed to file a pre-trial statement setting out his defence (as he was supposed to have done) meant even Massih appeared not to know what his client was going to say. Further, Bourgass's explanation for why the recipes were in his handwriting showed that he thought it was acceptable to use poison under some circumstances.

All Bourgass's questioning was conducted through an interpreter, with each question having to be translated into Arabic and Bourgass's replies then translated back into English. It was a long and drawn-out process with his cross-examination by the prosecution lasting for several days.

In his initial police interviews, Bourgass had claimed that he had found the poison recipes and some of the other suspect items in a sports bag that he'd picked up in the Brixton area of south London. Now, he had a different explanation. He hadn't found the items in Brixton, they had been brought to the Wood Green flat by Meguerba (to whom they belonged) for Bourgass to look after.

Bourgass said he had originally met Meguerba in north London when he had sold him some clothing. Later, Meguerba had come to the Wood Green flat and told Bourgass of his plan to use the recipes to help his countrymen poison the militia and Bourgass had agreed to help, with seemingly little persuasion.

Bourgass stuck to this explanation for the existence of the recipes, despite Sweeney's ridiculing the plan to use them against the Algerian militia as plainly unworkable. How, the prosecution barrister asked, were the villagers going to avoid poisoning themselves if they had laced the village's food supplies with deadly ricin or cyanide? Were they going to poison the food at the last moment, then? Would they have a lookout posted at the edge of the village, whose job was to shout 'Quick! The enemy are coming! Get cooking!'

Bourgass just shrugged and said Meguerba hadn't discussed the plan in detail.

Sweeney also challenged Bourgass as to why he had written the recipes out by hand, rather than simply photocopying them, if they had all come from a book that Meguerba had supplied. Bourgass's explanation was that the recipes had been drawn from different parts of the book, so it was simpler to write them out on one piece of paper than to photocopy all the different pages.

The prosecution went on to ask Bourgass about other items found at the flat. Bourgass either insisted that these belonged to Meguerba, and so weren't anything to do with him, or had an innocent explanation. The rubber gloves were, indeed, his – but were used for cleaning the flat. The thermometer was also his; he used it to check the outside temperature as he didn't like going out in the cold because of a bronchial problem. His explanation for the cherry stones and other seeds was that these were for making herbal remedies, rather than deadly poisons.

Despite his reliance on an interpreter, there were moments when it seemed that Bourgass's understanding of English was better than he was letting on. One of the prosecution's accusations was that the plotters had planned to smear poison on toothbrush heads, which would then be put back into shops for unsuspecting customers to buy. A number of new toothbrushes had been found at the flat, where the packaging had apparently been tampered with. When Sweeney made this suggestion, Bourgass grinned wryly, even before the interpreter had the time to translate the question.

The next defendant into the witness box after Bourgass was Mouloud Sihali, who was accused of being the plotters' Mr Fix-it. Sihali cut a very different figure from Bourgass: handsome, smartly dressed and with fluent English.

Sihali had longstanding links with David Khalef. For many years, he had shared Khalef's room at 240 High Road, Ilford. Khalef had been given the room in 1998 while his asylum claim was processed but often slept at the Finsbury Park Mosque, where he worked as a cleaner and cook. During his absences, he would also allow Mohammed Meguerba and another associate, Omar Djedid, to stay at 240. By spring 2002, Khalef had moved to Thetford in Norfolk to take a job and Meguerba, Djedid and Sihali would all three regularly stay in the cramped room at 240 High Road.

At around this time, Sihali had started renting his own flat in Elgin Road, about 20 minutes walk from 240, having fraudulently obtained housing benefit using the false name Cristophe Riberro. Sihali wanted to set up home so he could bring over his fiancée from France and began to gradually move his property across from 240. He was in no great hurry to move, however, and had agreed that, in the interim, Meguerba and Djedid could stay at Elgin Road.

The prosecution's case against Sihali revolved around his ties to Meguerba, the man that Bourgass had identified as the initiator of the poison plot and whose fingerprints had been found all over the recipes and other suspect items. Sihali had a history of sharing accommodation with Meguerba and had allowed him to stay at Elgin Road. The prosecution claimed that Sihali had procured Elgin Road as a safe house for Meguerba, a haven from where he could plot his terrorist attack.

The prosecution produced mobile-phone records showing hundreds of calls made between Meguerba and Sihali – many of only a few seconds duration. It also showed that, using the name Cristophe Riberro, Sihali had acted as company secretary to a business set up by Meguerba. The Crown argued that the company, Seven Roses, which supposedly sold sweets and chocolates, was really a front to launder money to fund terrorism.

Sihali was also implicated because of his longstanding links with David Khalef. After raiding 240, police had found their way to Khalef's new accommodation in Thetford, where they recovered a copy of the poisons recipe tucked into Khalef's suitcase. As Khalef's erstwhile flatmate (albeit in Ilford rather than Thetford), this also put Sihali under police suspicion.

There was also fingerprint evidence linking Sihali to a stash of stolen or doctored passports police had found at 240. Although Khalef admitted having the fake documents in his keeping, Sihali was charged with joint possession.

Sihali's barrister Michael Mansfield QC began his defence by showing photos of Sihali's family and asking about the girlfriends he'd had at various times. Mansfield's apparent aim was to try to humanise Sihali and undermine the prosecution portrayal of him as a ruthless and determined extremist. Tall and good looking, it was easy to think that Sihali would have no difficulty in attracting girlfriends.

Sihali was subject to detailed cross-examination by the prosecution over several days but despite the evidence supposedly ranged against him, remained confident and consistent throughout.

The prosecution had found no evidence linking Sihali to the recipes at the centre of its case. None of his fingerprints was found on them or on any of the suspect items. The recipe that Khalef had in his suitcase had been found at his Thetford accommodation and there was nothing to suggest it had ever been at the Ilford flat the pair of them shared. Sihali testified that he had never seen the recipes and didn't know anything about them.

The false passports would take more explaining. These documents had been well hidden at 240 High Road and it was only when the police had taken the room apart that they were discovered: in a padded envelope, inside a supermarket carrier bag, concealed in the base of the bed. Sihali's fingerprint was found inside the envelope, which the prosecution said showed he had handled them.

Sihali's explanation was that he had come across Khalef one day sitting in the kitchen of 240 with the passports. Khalef told Sihali he had been given the documents by a friend for safekeeping and passed them to Sihali to look at. When Sihali realised what they were, he was furious, telling Khalef to get rid of them as they would only spell trouble.

Sihali claimed that when he checked a day or two later, he found the envelope had gone from its hiding place in the kitchen, and so assumed Khalef had got rid of the documents. Instead, it seemed, Khalef had ignored Sihali's warning and moved the fake documents into the bed base – where the police unearthed them.

Even though Sihali wasn't above using fake identities when it suited him (he had used at least two, Cristophe Riberro and one other), he insisted that he had been alarmed at finding

Khalef in possession of false passports. Sihali said that having one or two false passports for your own use was one thing, having a stack of them was more serious.

Although Sihali clearly knew Meguerba, there was nothing to link him with the other man at the heart of the prosecution case, Kamel Bourgass. Indeed Bourgass, who was quite prepared to try to shift the blame from himself on to others as he had with Meguerba, had never mentioned either Sihali or Khalef in any of his statements.

However, Sihali's association with Mohammed Meguerba – whose fingerprints were also found all over the recipes and alleged poison-making equipment – would take some explanation. Unsurprisingly, Sweeney cross-examined him on this point for many days.

Sihali said he had been introduced to Meguerba in early summer 2002 by Omar Djedid, who knew Sihali's flatmate David Khalef from the mosque. Djedid and Meguerba, who both started staying at 240 and then the Elgin Road flat from late summer 2002, ran a small business venture together, selling sweets and chocolates from market stalls.

Djedid had previously escaped from immigration detention and didn't carry a mobile phone for fear of being tracked by the authorities. Therefore, according to Sihali, when Meguerba was looking for Djedid to work on one of the market stalls or to get access to one of the Ilford flats to sleep, he would ring Sihali instead. Sihali's explanation for the short phone calls was that this was Meguerba calling Sihali to ask: 'Can you let me in?' or 'Is Omar there?'

The prosecution spent a lot of time probing Sihali on his role as company secretary of Meguerba's Seven Roses business venture, with the obvious inference that it was a front for money laundering. Sihali certainly didn't seem to have received any money from his involvement: his bank account and credit card statements showed his finances were extremely limited. Although he had several credit cards, all had a low credit limit and Sihali was at pains to point out that he always paid off the required minimum sum every month.

It seems likely that he agreed to act as company secretary, partly for altruistic reasons, to do a fellow countryman a favour, and partly for selfish ones, to give extra credibility to his Riberro alias.

Police had found some of Meguerba's personal paperwork and a passport at Sihali's Elgin Road flat after the former fled the country. The prosecution barrister suggested that Sihali had rented the flat as a safe house where Meguerba could oversee the poison plot. Sihali insisted, however, that the other man was in the flat under sufferance. Sihali had taken on the flat so he could set up home with his fiancée but when he had subsequently discovered that Meguerba was planning to install his own fiancée at Elgin Road, Sihali responded by throwing him out. Certainly, judging by Sihali's scathing references to Meguerba, he seemed to have little respect for him.

Police had found various items at Elgin Road that interested them: a print-out of a web page featuring a speech by Osama bin Laden on a window sill; a diary in a bag belonging to Meguerba which seemed to include some kind of code. On one page of the diary, there were various figures, quoted as distances on a map, but when combined, proved to be a dialling code and phone number in Pakistan. The purpose of this was never fully explained, but the crude code was hardly James Bond stuff.

The prosecution tried to paint Sihali as the plot's Mr Fix-it because he had provided accommodation for Meguerba and support for his business venture. However, Sihali had no obvious ties with the other central figure, Kamel Bourgass, nor with the other supposed plotters, the teenager Sidali Feddag or Mustapha Taleb, from the mosque bookshop.

Sihali operated under a different moral code to most people, using false identities and making fraudulent benefit claims when it suited him. He was clearly capable of dishonesty, but did that make him a terrorist? Despite being given a grilling over several days, Sihali was consistent in his evidence, and confidently referred back to the interviews he had given police more than two years earlier.

When Mouloud Sihali eventually finished giving evidence, the court's attention turned to the other three defendants. However, each of their barristers was to rise in turn to say their client would not be giving evidence, after all. There was to be no opportunity for the jury to hear from Khalef, Taleb or Feddag directly, and instead the jurors would have to rely on their respective barristers' accounts of them and their actions.

Khalef had admitted that he was holding the stash of false passports hidden in the bed at 240 High Street, Ilford (Sihali was jointly charged with their possession on the basis of fingerprint evidence but denied they were anything to do with him). Khalef was implicated in the alleged plot, because his fingerprints were found on the poison recipe hidden in a suitcase at his accommodation in Thetford. However, there were no fingerprints linking him with any of the recipes left by Bourgass at Feddag's room in Wood Green.

Khalef was represented by Marguerite Russell and her description of him was hardly flattering. He was, she said, an illiterate illegal immigrant with an IQ of just 75 (equivalent to that of an average six year old). Indeed, Khalef's police interviews had been ruled inadmissible as evidence because his low intelligence meant he should have had an 'appropriate adult' with him to ensure he understood what was going on. He had become tearful and confused during police questioning; at one point asking what the word 'caution' meant.

Since his arrest and incarceration in Belmarsh high-security prison, Khalef had been on anti-depressant drugs and was suffering from mental health problems.

Khalef sat impassively, gazing into space, as Russell went through her description. He spoke little English and relied on an interpreter to explain what was happening. Khalef was always smartly dressed, in shirt and tie, and grey sports jacket that looked too small on his stocky frame. He had short, thick, black hair with a widow's peak and soft brown eyes. His tight jacket made him look like a stuffed bear.

Russell suggested Khalef was a simple man in all senses of the word. He had moved to Thetford to take a job in a meat-packing factory, which Sihali's brother, who lived locally, had helped him find. The jury was shown Khalef's application to the Thetford employment agency, which was barely legible and riddled with gaps and childlike mistakes.

Russell went through bank statements covering his time in Thetford. These showed that Khalef would take out several small sums of money on the same day. Russell explained that Khalef didn't have the foresight to know how much money he needed to get through a particular day, so would end up going back to the cash machine two or three times.

She said that Khalef had spent time drinking in a pub in Thetford – hardly the actions of a Muslin extremist. He had made friends in the area but his illiteracy meant he hadn't been able to enter their numbers into his own mobile phone and had had to ask them to do it for him. Russell sought to

paint her client as an innocent abroad but concluded her
defence without offering any explanation as to how Khalef
had come to have the poison recipes in his bag.

Next it was the turn of Sidali Feddag's barrister, Toby
Hedworth QC.

Feddag was the youngest defendant by far – just 17 at the
time of his arrest. He, too, was an illegal immigrant, having
been brought to the UK by his father in 2000. He had already
confessed to having a false passport for himself and of trying
to buy another one for his brother.

Feddag's alleged role in the plot was letting the lead
conspirator, Kamel Bourgass, stay at his bed-sit in 352b
High Road, Wood Green, and asking his father to bring
castor beans – the key ingredient for making ricin – over
from Algeria.

Hedworth stressed that there was nothing to suggest Feddag
knew about the poison recipes, as none of his fingerprints had
been found on them or any of the other suspect equipment.
In his police interviews, Feddag had been helpful and insisted
all along that the items seized by police from 352b belonged
to Bourgass.

Hedworth added that castor beans had many entirely
innocent uses, so nothing sinister could be read into Feddag's
father's agreeing to bring some over to the UK at Bourgass's
request. Castor beans are common in Algeria and are used
for everything from decorations to home remedies. To make
the point that they have many innocuous uses, Hedworth
produced a child's Barbie lip gloss which listed Ricinus
Communis – castor bean oil – as one of its ingredients. As
far as other ingredients were concerned, Hedworth went on,
was the prosecution suggesting that Bourgass had brought

home endless sacks of apples and urged his room-mate: 'Eat, Sidali! Eat!'?

The final defendant, Mustapha Taleb, was represented by Ben Emmerson QC, who said his client had also been on anti-depressants since his arrest. Unlike the other defendants, Taleb was in the country legally, having been granted asylum in 2001.

Taleb was in his early thirties but already balding. His close-cropped hair revealed a nasty-looking scar on his forehead and his face seemed hard and unreadable. Despite his villainous appearance, however, Taleb was accused of only a minor role in the plot. His fingerprint was found on the back of one of the recipes which had been photocopied at the Finsbury Park Mosque bookshop, where Taleb worked. The prosecution claimed that such a task would only have been trusted to a member of the plot's inner circle.

Taleb was arrested in a bank in Wood Green on 7 January 2002, two days after the police raid on Sidali Feddag's flat. When his room in nearby Alexandra Grove was searched, police found something else that interested them: a CD-Rom computer disc which held over 50 files. Most of the files were reports of atrocities and political unrest in Algeria, but one included basic details for making a remote-controlled explosive device. However, despite extensive investigation by computer experts, even though the disk had been loaded on to his computer, it could not be proved that Taleb had ever opened or looked at the file. Further, even the prosecution admitted that the information in the file wouldn't have been much use to a would-be bomber, even if he had looked at it, as the instructions were 'incomplete, illogical and incoherent, insufficient to enable such a device to be made'.[9]

The next strand in the defence case was to call experts to provide evidence giving an insight into Algerian politics and culture.

A statement was read out from an Algerian academic, Dr Rashid Massoudi, who said that Algeria had become an increasingly dangerous place, following the military coup in 1992. Dr Massoudi painted a picture of political upheaval, horrific massacres and widespread unrest. He wrote about an area known as the Triangle of Death – which included the Setif area that Bourgass claimed Meguerba had wanted to help defend with the poisons – and which was where many of the massacres had taken place.

Dr Massoudi explained that young Algerian men were fleeing the country in droves to avoid conscription. Many ended up in London, where they would often gravitate towards Finsbury Park, which had long been a magnet for Algerian men.

He went on to give a flavour of what life was like in the UK Algerian community. Young men would arrive illegally, often with very little money and nowhere to live. Newcomers would depend on help and support from other community members to survive and Dr Massoudi explained that there is a strong tradition of hospitality in the Algerian community. Those who are better off are expected to help those who are struggling even if they are barely acquainted. Even he and his wife had, on occasion, opened their own home to strangers who had turned up, desperate, on their doorstep.

Dr Massoudi's evidence suggested that the defendants having shared accommodation should not be seen as indicating great closeness or even trust between them. It could just have easily been because they felt a cultural obligation to provide help.

The final piece of defence evidence came from an expert on herbal medicines, who confirmed that there was a strong tradition in Arabic culture of using homemade remedies. The expert described how seeds from apples and other fruits are crushed and mixed with sugar to treat many minor ailments; castor oil beans were used as an emetic to relieve stomach problems. Her evidence suggested that there might not have been anything inherently sinister in the collecting of fruit seeds and stones or castor oil beans of the kind that had been found at the Wood Green flat.

The trial then entered its final phase with speeches from the prosecution and defence summing up their cases. As is traditional, the prosecution went first to allow the defence to have the last word before the jury.

Prosecution barrister Nigel Sweeney QC spent days outlining the evidence against each of the defendants in turn. Kamel Bourgass was the lead conspirator: he had written out the recipes; his fingerprints were all over the suspect equipment; he had asked Feddag to obtain castor oil beans (the main ingredient of ricin); and he had strong links with Mohammed Meguerba. Sweeney also talked about Bourgass's fleeing to Bournemouth after the raid on the Wood Green flat and his subsequent flight to Manchester, where he was arrested. What Sweeney didn't say – and what the jury would only discover after they had delivered their verdict – was that it was during his arrest that Bourgass had brutally murdered detective constable Stephen Oake.

Mouloud Sihali was described once again as the conspiracy's Mr Fix-it, a man of considerable intelligence who had arranged a safe house for Meguerba and who helped to establish Seven Roses as a front for money laundering. Sihali had proven connections with Meguerba and ready access to the false passports hidden in the bed base at the room in Ilford High Road.

David Khalef was a 'foot soldier', according to Sweeney. Despite his lack of intelligence, he was a trusted member of the conspiracy, given a set of deadly recipes for safekeeping. Khalef had admitted to hiding the passports at Ilford and, like Bourgass and Sihali, had undisputed connections with Meguerba.

The fourth defendant, Sidali Feddag had let Bourgass, the mastermind behind the plot, stay in his room in Wood Green. He had arranged for his father to bring over castor oil beans, and had helped save the fruit seeds needed to make cyanide.

According to Sweeney, Mustapha Taleb must have been a trusted member of the conspiracy to have been given the task of photocopying the recipes. He also had a suspicious CD-Rom which confirmed his terrorist leanings.

After Sweeney had run through the evidence against each defendant, it was the turn of the defence to speak.

Michel Massih, acting for Kamel Bourgass, went first. There were three main planks to Bourgass's defence: first, yes, Bourgass had written out the recipes at Meguerba's behest, but Meguerba had wanted to use the poisons in Algeria, not the UK, and then only for self-defence. Second, there was no evidence of either poisons or explosives being made at Wood Green. Third, Bourgass had fled after the raid on Wood Green because he was frightened. Fear, not guilt, had made him behave irrationally, including fleeing London and lying to the police in his interviews.

Next, Michael Mansfield spoke on behalf of Mouloud Sihali. He reiterated that Sihali knew nothing about the recipes and had no links with three of the supposed conspirators: Bourgass, Feddag or Taleb. His links with Meguerba were entirely innocent and, indeed, he had thrown Meguerba out of his Elgin Road flat after their disagreement over the latter's fiancée.

Marguerite Russell's summing up focused on David Khalef's limited intelligence: he was illiterate and mentally immature, a trusting soul who was easily used by others but certainly no terrorist conspirator.

Toby Hedworth stressed Sidali Feddag's youth, just 17 when he was arrested. If Feddag really was part of a gang led by Bourgass, how likely is it he would have asked the 'terrorist mastermind' to move out of the flat so Feddag's brother could stay there? The small quantities of pips and seeds Feddag had saved were nowhere near enough to manufacture cyanide and Feddag had genuinely believed Bourgass wanted them to make home remedies. Hedworth also reminded the court how cooperative the teenager had been in his police interviews, suggesting he had nothing to hide.

The final barrister on his feet was Ben Emmerson QC, acting for Mustapha Taleb. Emmerson had barely spoken during the rest of the trial but his summing up was easily the best closing speech of all the defence barristers, delivered with style and humour. He ridiculed the prosecution's idea of Kamel Bourgass as some kind of terrorist mastermind. With his half-baked kitchen-sink chemistry and total lack of precautions, Bourgass was hardly George Clooney with his meticulous planning in the film *Ocean's Eleven*, now was he? For a determined terrorist, Bourgass was remarkably cavalier about being arrested, as he had continued his prolific but petty shoplifting activities when he was supposedly planning a campaign of bombing and poisoning.

Emmerson said there was an innocent explanation for how Taleb's fingerprint had ended up on the back of one of the recipes: it simply meant he had shovelled the recipe through the photocopier at some point during his job at the mosque bookshop. There was nothing to suggest Taleb had even glanced at what he had been given to copy, said Emmerson.

When Emmerson sat down, it was the turn of the judge to sum up the case, setting out the evidence from both sides and explaining the legal points for the jurors to consider before reaching a verdict.

And then at last, it was the jury's turn. The eight men and three women (one juror was excused on the first day of deliberations for health reasons) faced a mammoth task. Reaching a verdict in such a complex and high-profile case was never going to be quick or straightforward. There are strict rules governing jury confidentiality (and Draconian punishments for breaking them) so none of the eleven could discuss any of their deliberations with friends or family – and nor can this aspect be covered in this book, for the same reason.

It would be their job to discuss and weigh every piece of evidence for each of the five defendants to determine its significance – inevitably a daunting and demanding task. Jurors were no longer allowed to use the Old Bailey cafeteria, but had to wait in a separate lobby for the jury usher to escort them to their room. Several days into their deliberations, the judge advised he would accept a majority jury verdict of ten-to-one. Still the jury continued to deliberate.

Finally, on 8 April 2005, after three weeks of deliberations, the jury had reached verdicts on every charge but one, and sent a note to the judge to that effect. A few minutes later, with the atmosphere in the courtroom incredibly tense, the exhausted-looking jurors were led back into court.

The five defendants were being held in the cells at the Old Bailey, as they waited for the verdict. Bourgass, the convicted police killer, was kept separately and was already resigned to spending many years in prison. Sihali, Khalef, Feddag and Taleb knew they could be facing up to 30 years in prison and tried to keep themselves distracted and calm by playing games of cards and dominoes. When the four were told the verdicts were in, however, any attempts at remaining composed were abandoned.

Initially, everything in the cell where the four were held went quiet for a few seconds, before Feddag became manic, talking non-stop. Taleb began laughing hysterically and teasing Khalef for having gone so pale. The colour had, indeed, drained from Khalef's face and his hands were shaking and he began swearing, repeatedly.

Mouloud Sihali recalls that his chest felt tight and he found it hard to breathe. 'My stomach was squirming. I had prayed all through the time the jury was deliberating and thought that if God exists, this is the time he should show me some mercy.'

Mustering as much composure as they could, the five defendants, including Kamel Bourgass, were escorted back into the packed courtroom. Word of the verdict had spread and the press box and public gallery were full.

The foreman stood and was asked to read out each verdict in turn: Mouloud Sihali; David Khalef; Sidali Feddag; Mustapha Taleb: not guilty of all charges. Kamel Bourgass: guilty of conspiracy to cause a public nuisance; jury unable to reach a verdict on the murder conspiracy charge.

As the foreman sat down, reaction from the four acquitted defendants and their barristers ranged from stunned shock to jubilation. Sihali looked to the heavens and clasped his hands together, and then visibly relaxed and smiled gently as each further not-guilty verdict was read out. Feddag threw back his head in relief. Taleb stared fixedly ahead as though stunned. Khalef barely reacted initially, and just looked bemused – although he recovered his voice fairly rapidly, making everyone jump when he roared 'God is Great!', as he was led back to the cells.

By contrast, Bourgass, who was already serving a life sentence for murdering DC Stephen Oake, showed no emotion and simply stared at the floor. His QC, Michel Massih, looked furious.

Still unaware of Bourgass's conviction for murdering a police officer at the time of his arrest, the jury was sent back by the judge to have a further attempt at reaching a verdict on the murder conspiracy charge. However, after another two days, they still had not reached a majority verdict. The judge called it a day and the jury was dismissed with no conclusion having been reached about whether Bourgass had, indeed, intended to murder.

By any measure, it was an anti-climactic end to a trial that had been one of the longest and most expensive in British judicial history. The arrests of the supposed ricin plotters had been seized on by UK and American politicians to justify both the so-called 'war on terror' and the invasion of Iraq. The trial had cost an estimated £20 million, had seen four months of prosecution evidence, and had lasted six months. However, after deliberating for the best part of three weeks, the jurors had acquitted four of the five defendants of all charges. They had convicted the fifth of the more minor charge only and been unable to reach a conclusion on the more serious charge.

As the jury was soon to find out, much of the real drama of the case had gone on behind the scenes. When they left the Old Bailey for the last time (having been excused by the judge from jury duty for the rest of their lives), one of the ushers whispered conspiratorially: 'Read the Daily Mail tomorrow, you'll be amazed at what you missed...'

2
The Road from Algeria to the UK

Like so many other young Algerian men in the 1990s, the five defendants in the ricin trial had found their way to Britain after fleeing their home country.

Since 1992, Algeria had been neither a safe nor stable environment for its young men. The country had been torn by civil war, sparked after the government cancelled the general election, when the Front for Islamic Salvation (FIS) looked set to win. After a coup by army generals, guerrilla groups emerged to fight against the military government. There followed atrocities on both sides, with civilians bearing the brunt of the bloodshed. Thousands of people died in often arbitrary purges by government forces or in indiscriminate killing by the guerrillas, aimed at striking fear into the populace. The Algerian secret police, the DRS (Department of Information and Security), would pick people up seemingly at random for questioning, torture, or worse. Many thousands of people simply disappeared.

As the country sank into chaos, life for ordinary people became increasingly difficult. Conscription was introduced. There was a rigid curfew to control the population and roadblocks were set up on major routes to restrict the movements of the guerrillas. Transport of all goods became extremely difficult and soon prices of even basic foodstuffs were spiralling. There were food queues and corruption was rife, with bribery of police, petty officials and even shopkeepers becoming commonplace. The country's economy was in dire straits, and with no work, thousands of dispirited young men were left idling on the streets of Algeria's cities.

Unsurprisingly, by the mid 1990s there was a steady flow of young Algerian men leaving the country in search of a better life. Among them was Mouloud Sihali, who left in 1997 to avoid conscription into the hated Algerian army. In Algeria, army conscripts are targeted as sympathisers by the anti-government rebel forces and deemed fair game. On the other hand, any man discovered deliberately avoiding the draft by the government is arrested and sent to military camp for two years and then given a further two-year posting in a particularly hard area. Deserters are treated in a similarly harsh fashion. According to Sihali: 'In my country, if you perform military service, it is either kill or be killed.'[1]

Rather than be conscripted, Sihali took the advice of one of his elder brothers to quit Algeria and join another brother who was living in Italy.

Sihali came from a big and happy family. He was born in the town of Boudouaou, about 20 kilometres from Algiers, and was one of 14 children, having five brothers and eight sisters. His father had worked away in a Citroen factory in France for some years in the 1970s, before getting a job in a Coca-Cola plant back in Algiers, eventually being forced to retire at the age of 70.

The Sihalis were a close knit and respectable family of Berber descent, proud of their heritage, as the Berbers were the original inhabitants of North Africa long before the coming of the Arabs. Sihali describes his childhood as idyllic.

As the youngest boy, he was doted on by his parents and older siblings, and family photos show him as a happy child, who spent much of his free time on the beach or swimming in the sea, which was only a couple of miles from the family home.

Although his father was a strict disciplinarian, Sihali could turn this to his advantage, in an early display of the wiliness that would be useful to him as an illegal immigrant. If one of his sisters was due a beating for causing trouble or breaking something, then Mouloud would take the blame and the punishment for her, in return for a little money for ice cream. Sihali was a good student and had passed his Baccalaureate (high school diploma) with excellent grades, before going on to computer college. However, Sihali decided to leave Algeria before completing the course to avoid the compulsory two-year military service forced on all Algerian men finishing full-time education.

Sihali travelled to Italy on a genuine 28-day tourist visa to visit his brother Amar. Once there, however, Amar advised Sihali to try the UK, which was believed to be more welcoming to immigrants than Italy, where Amar complained of little work and constant harassment by the authorities.

There was no obvious legal way for Sihali to enter the UK, as Algeria is not a member of the European Union, so when, after just a month in Italy, Sihali embarked on his journey to the UK, travelling via Milan and Calais, his brother had equipped him with a false Italian identity card.

In summer 1997, the 21-year-old Sihali arrived at the port of Dover, ready to start his new life as an illegal immigrant in the UK. No one asked for any ID on arrival, so he destroyed his fake identity card in Dover. By the time he had cleared the port area, Sihali had missed his bus connection to London and was forced to take the train to Victoria Station in the heart of the capital. His train ticket cost £17, almost a quarter of the total amount of money that Amar had given him.

Although Sihali was thrilled to be in London and to see some of its famous landmarks, within hours of his arrival it was clear how unprepared he was for life in the UK. He had nowhere to stay, he already missed his family, and prices of food and accommodation were shockingly higher than he had ever imagined: his little stock of cash would not last long.

By late afternoon on his first day, Sihali was feeling desperate and sought help from a stranger who looked to be a fellow countryman. He was in luck. The man was, indeed, Algerian, and told him to go to Finsbury Park in north London, an area which had become known as 'Little Algeria', because of the large numbers of his countrymen who were drawn there.

Finsbury Park is an unprepossessing residential area, with excellent transport links. It has long proved a magnet for the Algerian community, with numerous Algerian-run cafés and other small shops in nearby Blackstock Road. It is also home to the now notorious Finsbury Park Mosque, which in recent years has become linked to the firebrand Islamic preacher Abu Hamza al-Masri. However, when Sihali arrived in Finsbury Park in 1997, the mosque was as much a social club for itinerant Algerian men as a religious centre. It was the place where young men would meet, gossip, eat and swap information on likely jobs.

Fortunately for the homeless and all but penniless Sihali, the mosque operated an unofficial 'pray to stay' system. Provided they acted humbly and, outwardly at least, observed the rules of Islam, men with nowhere to live could sleep on the mosque's basement floor.

It was hardly an ideal arrangement for Sihali, but at least it gave him a toehold for his new life in the UK. At night, he slept at the mosque, in the day he began to find odd jobs, delivering leaflets or labouring on building sites. The work was irregular and poorly paid, but essential if he was to survive as an illegal immigrant. Sihali says: 'Without work, you had no food or shelter, not even the price of a cup of coffee. Most jobs we could get were menial work and paid £10 or £15 a day, maximum. Cash in hand, of course. Without any proper ID, there was no hope of getting proper employment. All my spare time was taken up with looking for work for the next day, just so that I could exist.'[2]

It was while Sihali was sleeping at the mosque that his path first crossed with that of another defendant, David Khalef.

Khalef had arrived in the UK in 1998, the year after Sihali. Although, like so many of his countrymen, Khalef had come looking for work, in order to be able to stay in the country he put in a claim for political asylum, falsely alleging that he feared political persecution in Algeria.

Khalef was a similar age to Sihali but, unlike him, had served his two-year conscription, albeit in the Algerian army catering corps rather than a fighting unit. Khalef had renamed himself David, as he thought it sounded more continental and sophisticated than his real name, Aissa. Aissa translates as 'Jesus' and is considered old-fashioned in Khalef's own country and would provoke derision from his compatriots.

By the time Khalef and Sihali met, Khalef was living in accommodation provided for him by the UK authorities while his asylum claim was processed. He lived in a room on the top floor at 240 High Road, Ilford, a run down suburb in northeast London. The room was small, with a steeply sloping ceiling which made it seem even smaller, a bed, a little cupboard and a wardrobe. The bathroom and kitchen were shared with several other tenants.

It wasn't much, but it was home. Having slept on the mosque floor himself when he first arrived in London, Khalef knew that any accommodation could be used as currency among Algerian immigrants. Khalef struck a deal with the obviously better-educated Sihali: in exchange for the latter's help with his asylum claim and everyday matters that Khalef's limited intelligence made difficult, Sihali could share the room at 240 High Road.

Sihali and Khalef were unlikely friends let alone room-mates, but the arrangement suited them both. Khalef had been provided with vouchers to buy food while his asylum claim was processed, but the supermarket where they were valid didn't sell Halal meat. So Sihali would buy the meat from the local market with his earnings, while Khalef bought the daily basics at the supermarket using the vouchers.

When they were both in the room overnight, Khalef would sleep in the bed, while Sihali slept on the floor. When Khalef was absent – as he often slept at the mosque where he worked – Sihali was left free use of the room to entertain his various girlfriends.

Whereas Sihali was self-assured, intelligent and fluent in several languages, Khalef had a low IQ, spoke only a smattering of English and was all but illiterate. For all their differences, however, the two men seemed to enjoy a brotherly relationship, with Sihali acting as the older sibling, keeping an eye out for Khalef in exchange for the accommodation.

Sihali's language skills and general savoir-faire had earned him a reputation in his community as someone to call on for help with translation or dealings with the authorities. Khalef, on the other hand, had few friends, preferring his own company, and had a childlike desire to please. Acquaintances soon became disenchanted with him when they realised that he was so dependent on them and understood so little. Faced with someone he saw as an authority figure, Khalef would try to cover up his lack of understanding, nodding sagely and smiling at what he hoped were appropriate moments.

Luckily for Khalef, the jobs open to illegal Algerian immigrants didn't require much skill or education. He did jobs around the mosque, as a general hand and cleaner, and he sometimes travelled out of London for extended periods to find cash-in-hand work, usually in the building or catering trades. For a while Khalef drew on his experience in the army catering corps and had rented a small kitchen in the mosque, selling low-price food to visitors. But the arrangement was short-lived when his lack of organisation and failure to adhere to hygiene standards caused a number of cases of food poisoning, and the franchise was taken away from him by the mosque trustees.

Khalef was keen to be seen as a 'good Muslim', hence his helping out at the mosque and offering hospitality to Sihali, and later Omar Djedid and Mohammed Meguerba, but he also drank alcohol and slept fairly indiscriminately with Western women.

Khalef had applied for asylum as a means of staying in the country legally, but when the time came for his case to be heard, he panicked and failed to turn up for two crucial appointments.

His claim was ultimately rejected, but as the asylum system was in such chaos the authorities failed to take any action to remove him. Despite his now illegal status, Khalef continued to have both use of the room at 240 High Road and to receive food vouchers, right up until the time of his arrest.

For Mouloud Sihali, who had slipped into the country illegally, while he was living entirely under the radar there was no prospect of any such state support or anything other than the most menial work. Around the end of 2000, Sihali's situation was helped when his cousin Omar Nait Atmane left his own genuine French passport behind after a visit. Here was an opportunity for Sihali to have an 'official' (if bogus) identity. He changed his cousin's picture to his own and adopted his cousin's name. With his new identity, Sihali was lifted out of the netherworld of cash-in-hand jobs and was able to find agency work as a silver-service waiter, including a stint at the prestigious RAC Club on Pall Mall.

Having fake or doctored ID papers was pretty much routine among many in the Algerian community: it went with the territory of being an illegal immigrant and was a simple necessity of a life lived in the shadows. The practice was rife and so unremarkable that Sihali was barely surprised when at one point he was brazenly approached in a café and asked if he wanted a false passport.

Gaining regular employment, opening a bank account, or renting accommodation required an accepted form of identity, usually a passport or driving licence, so a cottage industry manufacturing false identities had sprung up around the Blackstock Road area of Finsbury Park. The process was simple: supply a convincing name and address of choice, some suitable pictures and a relatively modest sum of money to the fixer, and a few days later a passport was ready for collection.

Without identity documents, it was impossible to obtain decent work or claim benefits. For most of the community, using their genuine passports was not an option, partly because it would reveal their illegal immigration status, but there were other reasons too.

The UK Algerian community had been infiltrated by informants working for both the Algerian and the British authorities. Informants who fed information back to the British were treated with disdain and were quickly named when discovered, but the community was far more worried about those working for the Algerian authorities than the British. The British might merely be interested in their immigration status, but back at home the Algerian secret police, the DRS, could arrest and torture their families or even make them disappear completely. An assumed identity was vital for your own safety and that of your family.

Despite now being able to use his new identity to get better work, by 2001 Sihali was deeply dispirited with life in London. He was tall and good looking and had had several European girlfriends, but the relationships could never develop because he didn't dare tell them about his immigration status, or even his real name. He usually pretended to be a French migrant, but this had backfired on him spectacularly when one of his long-term girlfriends had wanted to marry him to get status in the UK for herself. Mortified, he had finished the relationship immediately without ever telling her the true reason.

Sihali felt trapped. He could never go back home without the risk of arrest and two years forced national service. In London, he had only the use of the floor in Khalef's tiny room to sleep on. The silver-service waiting was a step up from the more menial work he had been doing, but he yearned for a decent living standard and not to have to lie constantly and answer to a strange name.

Later that year, it seemed a solution had suddenly presented itself, when Spain announced an amnesty for illegal immigrants and a chance to earn Spanish citizenship. Sihali travelled to Spain twice in 2001: once to fill in the paperwork and a second time in September to sign the forms in the presence of a solicitor. On both occasions he met up with one of his brothers and stayed in Granada, where he had struck up a friendship with two men who owned a coffee bar. They were more than generous, giving him help and a roof over his head, and ferrying him around the city when he needed transport. One of the men, hearing that false identification was easier and cheaper to obtain in the UK than in Spain, had given him several hundred pounds to buy a passport and a driving licence. Sihali took the money and made a show of agreeing to help, but back in the UK he decided he ought not to risk involvement and returned the money.

Sihali's dream of Spanish citizenship in his own name was to be short-lived, scuppered, ironically, by problems over his different identities. Sihali's brother had brought Mouloud's genuine Algerian passport to show the solicitor in Granada, but there was no record of a Mouloud Sihali ever having entered the country as he had used the doctored Omar Nait Atmane passport to travel on both occasions. Sihali's claim was duly rejected and, deflated, he prepared to return to the UK.

In his despondency, Sihali had confused the times of his flight and missed his plane. His rescheduled flight was a few days after 9/11 and Sihali had first learned about the Al-Qaeda attacks on America during the flight home. He was deeply disturbed by the reports and decided it was fate that had stopped him getting citizenship in Spain and that he should make the best of life in the UK.

Once back in London, Sihali threw himself into his waiting jobs and, by February 2002, had saved up enough money to buy a forged passport. He chose the name Cristophe Riberro, because he thought it was ambiguous enough to cover several nationalities. A benefits officer had advised Sihali that he was entitled to claim help towards housing costs as his wages were so poor. Armed with the new passport and the hope of extra benefit cash, Sihali set about finding somewhere of his own to rent. By the summer of 2002, he had found a small but comfortable flat in Elgin Road, Ilford, about 20 minutes' walk from Khalef's room. He began to move some of his belongings to the new address, but decided to take his time before moving in fully.

The Elgin Road flat was to be a new start and somewhere to call his own. Sihali also hoped it might make a home for a wife, as he had been in discussions about marrying the sister of his cousin, Omar Nait Atmane, whose passport he had adopted.

There was another reason why Sihali wanted his own place: David Khalef had started to allow other acquaintances to use the room at 240 High Road.

By late spring 2002, Khalef was once again working outside London. With the help of another one of Sihali's brothers, Farid, Khalef had found work in Norfolk. Khalef had registered with several employment agencies using a false French passport that he had bought in Blackstock Road. In his naivety, he had used his own name, David Khalef, and his own birthday on the forged document, so that he wouldn't forget them if challenged. Through the agencies, he found work in various food factories around Thetford, cleaning and gutting chickens, preparing pork and packing meat products. By the summer, Khalef was well settled and living in a house in Ethel Coleman Way, Thetford, sharing his twin-bedded room with a Portuguese man. While he was out of London, Khalef had agreed that two other Algerians could also have use of his room in Ilford: Omar Djedid and Djedid's business partner, Mohammed Meguerba. Both men were to have pivotal roles in the subsequent unfolding of the ricin plot.

Omar Djedid's immigration status was even more precarious than that of Khalef (who had been untroubled by the authorities, despite his asylum claim being rejected in 1999). Djedid was on the run from the British authorities, after escaping from Yarl's Wood detention centre in Bedfordshire in February 2002. Djedid had been detained after returning to the UK from Chechnya, where he claimed to have been offering medical aid to the Islamic rebels.

However, after being held for several months, he had managed to escape in the confusion that ensued after a fire at the centre. Once the smoke detectors had been triggered, all doors at the centre were opened automatically and Djedid simply walked out.

He made his way back to London, where he met up with David Khalef, whom he knew from previous spells in the Finsbury Park area. Djedid often disappeared without explanation, so his sudden reappearance didn't raise any suspicions. Unaware that Djedid was wanted by the authorities, Khalef agreed to let him stay at 240 High Road. Within a few weeks, Djedid had brought his business partner, Mohammed Meguerba, to the room in Ilford and introduced him to Khalef. Mouloud Sihali came home one day to find both Meguerba and Djedid at 240 – and that Khalef had agreed they could both stay there while he went to work in Norfolk.

Soon Djedid and Meguerba were sleeping at 240 fairly regularly, but Sihali was increasingly unhappy about the arrangement, which he had not been consulted about. Sihali began acquiring furniture for his new address in Elgin Road (at one point, Meguerba helped him move in a washing machine he had bought) and with the three of them in Khalef's tiny room, conditions were almost intolerable.

Occasionally the two newcomers would use a spare room in the house to sleep, but the other residents of the multi-occupancy house were getting less tolerant of their use of the shared kitchen and bathroom. Sihali was also aware that if the landlord paid a surprise visit, then Khalef would be in trouble for letting others use the room. To defuse the situation, Sihali agreed that Djedid and Meguerba could use his newly acquired flat in Elgin Road. It was an act of generosity which was to have severe consequences for Sihali when Meguerba was identified as the instigator of the ricin plot, along with his fellow conspirator Kamel Bourgass.

Despite his reservations about them, Sihali agreed to help Meguerba and Djedid in other ways. The pair ran a reasonably successful business, selling sweets at various markets around London. Meguerba wanted to apply for a trading licence, to secure regular and better positioned pitches at the markets. To this end, he had set up a company, Seven Roses, which meant he needed someone to be listed as company secretary. Although Djedid worked with him on the stalls, he was in no position to get involved in the licence application, for fear of being tracked by the immigration authorities after his escape from detention. So Djedid asked Sihali if he would do the honours – which Sihali agreed to do, using his Cristophe Riberro alias.

Sihali had never especially liked Meguerba and his agreeing to help was not simply an act of duty or altruism. He was also motivated by the hope that being listed as a company director would give credibility to his recently acquired false identity.

Whatever Sihali's intentions, his actions were given an entirely different and sinister construction during the trial, with the prosecution claiming Seven Roses was a front for the laundering of money raised for terrorism.

While much is known about the four acquitted defendants in the ricin trial, the convicted murderer Kamel Bourgass – the sole defendant to be found guilty at the ricin trial – remains mysterious. His stated name, nationality and age changed many times during his various police interviews. It seems most likely he is an Algerian, but he has claimed at various times to be Tunisian or Moroccan. He used various other identities during his time in London including El Mouatez ('the saintly one') and Omar Rami, as well as Nadir Habra, which – to the surprise of his own barrister – he announced to be his 'real name' during the ricin trial. He also had a false passport in the name of Hans, which was found during the police search of a self-storage facility in Wembley, west London.

Bourgass claimed at the trial that he came into the port of Dover on 30 January 2000, via Calais, smuggled through in the back of a lorry. Like Mouloud Sihali, he said he had simply walked into Dover station, boarded a train to London, and eventually found his way to Finsbury Park. The day after his arrival, like David Khalef, Bourgass claimed asylum, going to the immigration offices in Croydon to file his case. At the time, there was a huge backlog in the processing of asylum claims and, rather than his application being processed immediately, Bourgass was given temporary accommodation in Manchester while he waited to hear.

By August 2001, Bourgass was notified that his claim had been rejected, but instead of being deported immediately, he was told to report to an immigration office once a month. An appeal was lodged against the dismissal, and although it was heard in November 2001, Bourgass did not attend: he had already dropped off the radar, eventually turning up back at Finsbury Park. His appeal was formally dismissed in December.

Bourgass claimed to have had brief spells of employment as a waiter in a pizza restaurant and as a street cleaner, but these jobs would hardly account for the £4,100 found in his bag at Wood Green. It seems more likely that this money was the proceeds from his thievery.

Bourgass was a prolific and not always successful thief. In July 2002, he had been arrested for stealing jeans from a shop in Romford, Essex. He refused to give an address and stated he was an illegal immigrant, giving his name to the arresting officers as Nadir Habra. The police requested an immigration official to interview Bourgass while they had him in custody, but no one was available. The immigration authorities advised the police to issue an IM3 form, which meant that Bourgass could be considered by a court for detention or deportation, but instead he was taken to Havering Court, fined £70 and then released. The immigration authorities were never informed, so Bourgass was free to return to Finsbury Park, triggering a sequence of events that would lead ultimately to the discovery of the so-called ricin plot and the brutal killing of DC Stephen Oake.

Before his arrest for shoplifting, Bourgass had been befriended by the teenager Sidali Feddag, whom he had met at the mosque. The 15-year-old Sidali Feddag had arrived in the UK in November 2000 with his father. Feddag was a good school student and, despite his youth, was wise enough to realise he had no future in his home city of Algiers, where there was little hope of work or earning a decent living.

One of five children, Feddag was mature for his age, highly resilient and clear about what he wanted for his future. He had travelled to France on several occasions with his father, a minor airport official, and knew what European countries had to offer: freedom and excitement and, most importantly, a good standard of living. Before long, he had persuaded his father to let him leave Algeria to take his chances in Europe. The pair briefly considered France, but the Feddags were worried about French racism towards Algerians, so they settled on the UK as their destination. Britain was seen as far more tolerant of immigrants than most EU countries and as providing them with better opportunities.

Although Feddag's mother was against the idea of her teenage son's leaving, Sidali quietly obtained a tourist visa and in late 2000, he arrived in the UK with his father. The pair went immediately to visit a family friend in Leyton, east London, and, after three days, Feddag senior returned home to explain to his distraught wife that her son was now in the UK in the care of their friend. By December, Feddag's older brother, Mouloud, had also joined him in London.

Feddag stayed in Leyton for five months, before moving to Stamford Hill in north London to work as a street cleaner, using a false identity card he had bought. His brother had discovered that large numbers of their countrymen congregated in the Finsbury Park area and became a regular visitor there. Sidali Feddag soon followed his brother's lead and moved shortly afterwards to nearby Haringey.

Like Kamel Bourgass and David Khalef, Feddag decided the best way to stay in the UK was to claim political asylum, and so he visited a firm of local solicitors to register his claim. With the necessary paperwork in hand, he approached Haringey council in July 2001. Feddag claimed he was a penniless asylum seeker with nowhere to live. The council put him up in a hotel for a few months and then in September 2001, while his claim was still waiting to be processed, he was given a room at 352b High Road, Wood Green, a few miles north of Finsbury Park. Living on food vouchers and unable to work legally because of his asylum-seeker status, Feddag had a lot of time on his hands and spent much of it around Finsbury Park, playing football or hanging around the mosque.

Meanwhile, Feddag's parents were becoming concerned about their still young son. They made frequent attempts to speak to him on the phone via their family friend in Leyton, but the friend was forced to admit he rarely saw Feddag any more. The friend began to encourage Feddag to visit more often so that he could at least pass some news back to his worried parents. So Feddag began to stay at the Leyton flat more frequently, rather than trek back to his room in Wood Green, and at other times he would sleep on the mosque floor if it was too late to get home. On these occasions, he would usually see another man who seemed to sleep at the mosque permanently and called himself 'Nadir', aka Kamel Bourgass.

In the post-9/11 climate, the use of the mosque as an unofficial hostel for young men was increasingly attracting suspicion and criticism. In December 2001, prompted by concerns about damage to the mosque's reputation, its trustees brought the practice to an end.

To Feddag, Bourgass seemed quiet and easy going, and unlikely to cause any trouble, so he offered him the use of the room in 352b Wood Green. Feddag's brother Mouloud was still staying there intermittently but, as he had a night job in a bakery, Mouloud would sleep there during the day, leaving Bourgass the use of the bed at night.

Bourgass did not have a job, as such, but he made a reasonable living by variously stealing clothes to sell on and shoplifting indiscriminately (or 'shopping for free' as Feddag was to describe it in the trial). He had developed various methods of beating the shops' security systems, but he also stole completely useless items at times, including a stack of dishwasher powder that sat unused in 352b for many months. However, as far as the Feddags were concerned, Bourgass was little bother: he went out a lot and rarely spoke to Sidali Feddag, only briefly discussing his family and talking about religious matters maybe once or twice.

The most notable thing about Bourgass was that he seemed to suffer with his stomach. He would endlessly be making herbal remedies for his various ailments from ingredients he kept in his personal section of the room's wardrobe. He scoffed when Feddag admitted he knew nothing of these remedies and told how his grandmother had taught him their use. When Bourgass asked if Feddag's father could bring over castor oil beans from Algeria when he next visited, Feddag thought little of it: castor oil beans were commonplace at home and were another of grandmother Bourgass's home remedies, as far as he was concerned. However, it was these castor oil beans which the anti-terror police were later to claim were being stockpiled to make the deadly poison ricin.

In December 2002, the Feddags' family friend left Leyton for an extended visit to Algeria. His mother had recently died in the UK and had wanted to be buried in her home country. The friend flew her body back and organised her funeral, which took several weeks. As there had been a burglary in the flat downstairs recently, he asked Sidali Feddag to house-sit while he was away.

There were other changes, too, at the end of 2002. Feddag's brother, Samir, was due to come to the UK, and Feddag asked Bourgass to move out of 352b: three people in the room would have been too crowded. Bourgass agreed, but asked to leave some of his possessions in the room for safekeeping. It seemed a small thing to ask and Feddag readily agreed, but it was to prove a fateful decision when the anti-terror police searched the property a few weeks later.

So, in December 2002, Bourgass moved out of 352b, leaving behind various bags and what Feddag thought were herbal remedies. Feddag's brother Samir duly arrived and moved in. He, like Mouloud and Sidali before him, was respectful of Bourgass's property and left his belongings untouched – a courtesy that almost certainly saved Samir Feddag from facing a conspiracy to murder charge alongside his brother.

Unlike the other acquitted defendants, Mustapha Taleb was in the UK legally. He had arrived in the country in 2000 after living in Germany and Morocco for brief periods and immediately made an apparently legitimate claim for political asylum. His body showed obvious signs of physical abuse, including heavy scarring to his head, which Taleb says was a result of torture during interrogation by the DRS, the Algerian secret police.

Taleb was born in 1969 in the town of Tlemcen, in the northwest of Algeria, close to the Moroccan border. Many natives of this area are much paler skinned than most Algerians and are of Jewish appearance. Taleb himself was often mistaken for a Jew when he lived in London due to his full beard and long hair: his landlord initially mistook him for a high-ranking rabbi because he did not wear a skullcap.

Taleb was a modest, quiet and intelligent man who had trained in engineering at university, but the lack of jobs in the chaos of post-coup Algeria had forced him down another career path and he had become a government tax inspector. His government employment had exempted him from compulsory conscription into the army, but it hadn't prevented him from being picked up randomly by the DRS and subjected to harsh interrogation and torture.

This was routine practice for the DRS: no one was above suspicion and everyone was liable to sudden arrest on the merest hint that they might be connected with the rebels. Taleb had been an open supporter of the Front of Islamic Salvation opposition party in the past and admits that he helped send clothes and supplies to the families who had fled to the mountains after the 1992 coup. He insists, however, that he had no links with any violence, an assertion given weight by the fact that he was released after interrogation.

On his release, Taleb fled to another Algerian city to lie low, but was spotted by an old neighbour from his hometown and reported to the authorities. Fearing further arrest and torture, Taleb left Algeria. For a while, he lived in the enclave of Melilla on the Moroccan coast, an autonomous city belonging to Spain, hoping to become a Spanish citizen eventually. Unfortunately, his passport expired before he had been there long enough to qualify for citizenship and he didn't dare renew it for fear of alerting the Algerian authorities to his whereabouts. He left Melilla and eventually landed in the UK, where his asylum claim was duly processed and he was granted the right to stay.

Taleb inevitably drifted towards the community in Finsbury Park and found a job in a butcher's shop on Blackstock Road. After a while, he befriended the owner of the franchise to the bookshop in the Finsbury Park Mosque, Nasreddine Fekhadji.

The bookshop owner, Fekhadji, was in poor mental and physical health. He was on strong prescription drugs but often forgot to take them and became severely confused and agitated when not sufficiently medicated. Fekhadji had run the small bookshop more as a disorganised supermarket, selling toiletries and snacks alongside copies of the Koran and scholarly texts. Taleb agreed to help out and started to transform the shop, importing books, CDs and tapes from France on the political situation back at home. One of his duties was to operate the public photocopier at the mosque, something which was to land him in trouble when his fingerprint was found on a photocopy of the Bourgass poison recipes.

The Algerian men who ended up in the dock alongside Taleb in the ricin trial were a disparate group, loosely linked via the Finsbury Park Mosque. The links between them all were tenuous at best: Mouloud Sihali and David Khalef had shared a genuine, if unlikely, friendship. Sihali had agreed to act as company director to Meguerba's business venture, partly because of the cultural obligation to help a fellow countryman, partly to try to make his own false identity seem more authentic. Feddag had allowed Bourgass use of his room at 352b High Road. Sihali and Khalef had never met Feddag and their only link was through Bourgass's association with Mohammed Meguerba.

The five were largely thrown together by need and circumstance and the cultural obligations of hospitality. Most had not set eyes on each other until they were remanded to Belmarsh prison before trial (as a convicted murderer, Kamel Bourgass was held separately).

The Algerian community of which they were part operated on an odd combination of mutual suspicion and implicit trust, which jars with Western sensibilities. You were expected to throw open your home to someone you barely knew, but not to ask them many questions. Thus men could be sharing rooms and even beds on a rota basis without being friends or otherwise having much to do with each other.

Individuals were often known by a single first name to preserve anonymity. If a full name were overheard, the fear was it would be reported by spies to the DRS, causing problems for a man's family back in Algeria. Asking a family name would be seen as over-inquisitive or insulting. Further, in the closely-knit community back home, last names were rarely used because everyone knew everyone else. To avoid confusion, a nickname or place of origin might be tacked on to the first name, and this practice continued in the UK. For example, because he ate so much, Mustapha Taleb's brother was known as 'Lacoste', after the crocodile logo used by the French clothing brand of that name.

Bourgass was a dedicated and prolific thief, but for the others, low-level criminality was just part of the everyday life of an illegal immigrant. (As already mentioned, Taleb was the only one of the five in the country legally and allowed to work.) The Algerians did not see themselves as criminals and adhered to their own moral code, albeit one that may seem bizarre to an outsider. Sihali and Khalef were regulars at the mosque, but both drank alcohol and had European girlfriends. Sihali fiddled the benefits system, but took great pride in paying off his credit card bills each month; he held two fake passports but refused to obtain a false ID for his Spanish associate and was furious when he found David Khalef with the envelope full of bogus documents.

For many in the Algerian community, law breaking was a simple matter of expediency or survival. The problem for the four acquitted defendants was that, in the heightened atmosphere post-9/11, activities like holding false passports would take on a far more sinister construction. It was a change which would ultimately lead to their being accused of conspiracy to murder in the biggest terrorist trial the UK had ever seen.

3
Everything Changes on 9/11

The attacks on America on 11 September 2001 led to an immediate change in the political climate that went far beyond just the United States itself. US president George W. Bush rapidly declared a 'war on terror', to destroy Al-Qaeda and track down Osama bin Laden. The Americans took both military and economic action against states suspected of harbouring terrorist organisations. The US intelligence agencies were set to work to disrupt Al-Qaeda, and the newly passed Patriot Act, pushed through only six weeks after the 9/11 attacks, was a key weapon in their armoury. The act gave the state extended powers to monitor phone calls and emails and greater access to financial and other records.

Like their American counterparts, the British intelligence services abruptly shifted their counter-terror focus to Al-Qaeda. Given Al-Qaeda's reach around the globe, intelligence sharing between states and global surveillance became increasingly vital intelligence tools.

At the time when Western governments were waking up to the threat from Islamic extremists, the Algerian authorities were seeking to ingratiate themselves with the West after years in the political wilderness. The US in particular had previously been fiercely critical of Algeria's appalling record on human rights. However, Algeria had vast resources of natural gas and oil, which would solve many of its economic problems, providing it could court investment from Europe and America.

In an attempt to mend fences between itself and the West, Algeria offered to provide intelligence information, emphasising the supposed links between Al-Qaeda and the rebel forces fighting its own government. In the aftermath of 9/11, the US was keen to develop new allies. So in December 2002, US Assistant Secretary of State William Burns visited Algiers and smoothed the way for the resumption of diplomatic relations. Washington promised the Algerians increased aid and military equipment as part of the process of intensifying security cooperation between the two countries.

The Algerians were keen to deliver on their side of the bargain and rapidly supplied the names of 350 nationals allegedly linked to Al-Qaeda, some of whom were living in the UK.

British intelligence services were veterans at handling terrorist threats after decades of dealing with the IRA and other Irish Republican terror organisations. The problem with Al-Qaeda was that it was a completely different animal: whereas the IRA was a hierarchical organisation, run along military lines, Al-Qaeda had no clear structure, which made it harder to infiltrate and disrupt. Originally formed from the mujahadeen veterans who had fought the Soviet army in Afghanistan, Al-Qaeda was now almost a terrorist franchise and its membership was fluid, with many disparate radical groups from as far apart as North Africa and Pakistan coming together under its umbrella.

The 9/11 attacks had caused almost as many reverberations in the UK as they had in America, amid concerns that

Britain, with its 'special relationship' with the US and strong support for the Gulf war was also a likely Al-Qaeda target. In an echo of the US Patriot Act, the British government rushed through legislation to deal with the increased terrorist threat. The 2000 Terrorism Act was replaced by the Anti-Terrorism, Crime and Security Act (ATCSA), which was introduced to parliament on the 19 November 2001 and became law within a matter of weeks. Part four of the act was a controversial provision to detain foreign nationals resident in the UK, if the Home Secretary simply *suspected* them of terrorist activities. Between their introduction in 2001 and 2003, 17 men were rounded up and held in Belmarsh prison under these provisions. These so called 'Belmarsh Powers' were widely criticised as there was no onus on the Home Secretary to charge the detained men or to bring them to trial. To pass legislation which treated foreign nationals differently from British-born suspects, the British government was forced to derogate from the European Convention of Human Rights.

The UK was unable to deport the Belmarsh detainees because of a 1996 European Court of Human Rights decision (*Chahal v UK*), which ruled out deportation where a prisoner faces significant threat of torture if returned to his home country.

If the Belmarsh detainees couldn't be deported, the Home Office argued that the threat to national security they presented meant they had to be held indefinitely without charge. It was an unprecedented position for the British government to adopt – and one which was overthrown by the House of Lords in 2004. The Lords were to describe the Belmarsh powers as 'anathema', and incompatible with European laws on human rights.

Another effect on Britain of the 9/11 attacks was to fuel public and official mistrust of immigrants, particularly British-based Muslims. The French security forces had long been critical of Britain's perceived apathy towards radical Muslims, warning that London was becoming a fundraising and recruitment centre for extremists. Before 9/11, it is believed that an unofficial understanding, known as the covenant of security, had existed between the British authorities and leaders of its Muslim communities. The understanding was that Islamists were bound by conventions of hospitality and teachings of the Koran not to take direct action against a host country. The British authorities would take a hands-off approach towards the Muslim community on the understanding that it would self-police any radicals among it. However, if it ever existed, this strategy came to an abrupt end following the 2001 attacks on America.

Even before 9/11, illegal immigration had long been a hot political issue in the UK, with the tabloid press regularly running stories about 'porous borders', and politicians of all parties believing there were votes to be had in being tough on 'bogus asylum seekers'. Over the preceding years, there had been attempts to clamp down on numbers of entrants by the crude expedient of making it as difficult as possible for people get to the UK, regardless of whether they were genuinely persecuted in their home country. As a result, for the likes of Mouloud Sihali and David Khalef, desperate to escape the political turmoil of Algeria, there simply was no way of getting into the UK legally.

Overnight after 9/11, Muslims in Britain came under greater suspicion. Behaviour long associated with the Algerian community around Finsbury Park – illegal entry, with its resulting wariness towards outsiders, use of false identities, and black-market working – was suddenly cast in a new light and seen as potential evidence of terrorist activity.

The Algerians themselves hadn't previously paid much attention to Western media – Sihali only learned of the attacks on America a few days later – and even post-9/11, they were too preoccupied with day-to-day survival to take much interest in the ensuing political debate in Britain. However, the men could not fail to notice the change in the way they were perceived in the aftermath of the attacks.

On his return to London from Spain soon after 11 September 2001, Sihali found that people who had previously been friendly were now distrustful. Sihali does not wear traditional Muslim garb but found that his olive skin was enough to make him suspect. 'There was no real open hostility, but I could feel people's suspicion of me. The way they looked at me had changed', he says.[1]

Mustapha Taleb faced more open antagonism, which was enough to scare him into trimming his previously long beard and abandoning Arab robes for Western dress. Plenty of other Algerians did the same, also for fear of reprisals, he says.

The Finsbury Park Mosque – an unprepossessing building on a residential street – became a target for abuse, often attracting hostility from fans on their way to the nearby Arsenal football stadium. On one occasion a lorry load of building rubble was dumped outside the mosque.

The Algerians were undoubtedly unnerved by the changes they experienced, but life had to go on. Day-to-day life as an illegal immigrant was difficult anyway, and the increased suspicion was just another difficulty that had to be worked around. Most kept their heads down as much as possible and hoped that life would carry on much as usual. Work had still to be found, accommodation sorted out, food bought.

Most still had no desire to return home to Algeria – because of concerns for their safety or for economic reasons – so the trade in false identity papers, the use of assumed names and the making of false asylum claims continued unchanged. Even if any of them had had the political nous to realise that post-9/11 such activities would be seen in a more sinister light, they wouldn't have thought there was much they could do about it.

Given that so much of the suspicion that would engulf the defendants flowed from their illegal status, on the face of it, it seems surprising that they didn't make every effort to regularise their presence in the UK. For most of them, there was no legal means of entering the country (the exception being 15-year-old Sidali Feddag who arrived on a tourist visa with his father) but, once arrived, they may have had more options than they realised. According to one leading immigration lawyer, the level of political turmoil and human rights abuses which continued to prevail in Algeria at the time meant that many Algerians could legitimately show grounds to remain in the UK.[2]

The defendants, through a combination of lack of knowledge, deeply ingrained fear of officialdom and lack of easy access to expert legal advice, did little to attempt to change their illegal status. Sihali didn't even bother to apply for asylum and Feddag applied but didn't see the process through.

Despite the change in political climate, the men carried on doing what was necessary to scratch a living. If there was no work and money was tight, a group of them would club together to buy a loaf, perhaps a little meat and a bottle of soft drink. They'd sit in nearby Finsbury Park, share the provisions and watch life go by. If someone had a room, it would provide accommodation for as many people who could fit on the floor for the night. For those with nowhere else to stay, there was always the option of sleeping on the basement floor of the mosque.

Mouloud Sihali gives some indication of how Algerian mores governing hospitality are often misunderstood in the West. He says: 'Europeans just don't understand the way the Algerian mind works. We were all in the same tight situation. Everyone mucked in to help one another, personal friend or not. If you had food, drink, cigarettes, coffee, a room, then it was a moral obligation to share. If you had a mobile phone and someone asked to make a call, you lent it to them.'[3] The fact that men shared accommodation or helped each other in other ways did not necessarily signify that they knew each other well or had any kind of close friendship. However, with all the links between community members, it's unsurprising that the security services were able to tie so many men together into a bigger conspiracy when they disrupted the ricin plot.

Another result of 9/11 was to put the mosque which was at the heart of the north London Muslim community under greater scrutiny, with the authorities becoming particularly interested in any possible links to Al-Qaeda. Attention began to focus on the firebrand imam who preached there on a Friday: Mostafa Kamel Mostafa, better known to the UK public as Abu Hamza.

Hamza was a gift bogeyman to the British tabloid press. Blind in one eye and using a hook in place of one of the stumps that are all that are left of his arms, the Egyptian-born former civil engineer appeared almost a cartoon-like villain. But there was real menace behind the facade. Hamza claims he lost his hands and left eye in Afghanistan, when he was the victim of a landmine explosion; his detractors say he was maimed when mixing explosives in a terrorist training camp. In any event, after the accident in 1993, he returned to Britain fired with the idea of spreading jihad, war against the non-believers of Islam, and became a keen student of the notorious preacher Abu Qatada. By 1997, Hamza had been appointed the Khateeb (Friday preacher) at Finsbury Park Mosque, wooing the management committee of mosque trustees with his passion, knowledge of spiritual matters and seemingly the fact that he demanded only the price of a dinner for his services in delivering the Friday sermon.

According to some observers, Hamza was not a particularly gifted orator, although there was a certain fire and panache to his sermons; nor was he as knowledgeable of the Koran as his mentor Abu Qatada (with whom he later had an acrimonious falling out). One advantage he had was that he spoke good English, which meant he could preach to the congregation at Finsbury Park Mosque, even though it was drawn from many different nationalities. Audiences were drawn to Hamza because his sermons were accessible; he spoke in simple down to earth terms rather than using scholarly concepts. Usually, there was standing room only at his sermons.

Despite his popularity among his followers, within a year the mosque trustees were to rue their appointment of Hamza, as his behaviour was becoming more erratic and his rhetoric more extreme. However, by this time, Hamza's position at the mosque was firmly entrenched, surrounded as he was by an inner circle of fervent supporters. When an informal attempt to oust Hamza failed, the trustees turned to legal action. Despite spending over £14,000 on lawyers' fees, they still didn't manage to get him out. Finally in 1999, the trustees conceded to let Hamza stay in exchange for a promise that he only preached on two Fridays a month.

During this period, the British authorities' attitude towards Hamza seems to have been ambivalent. Both the police and MI5 had reportedly been courting him independently since 1997 in the hope he would become an informant. Hamza strung both organisations along, initially appearing willing to cooperate, but never actually delivered any useful information. However, the result of his courting by the authorities was that Hamza was left largely undisturbed to carry on his secret jihadi recruitment operations. By 1998, the authorities were beginning to realise that Hamza might be a serious threat, rather than just a rabble-rousing fantasist, and he was warned by his MI5 contacts that he was 'walking a tightrope'.[4]

In December 1998, 16 Western tourists were kidnapped in Yemen in retaliation for the arrest in Yemen of Hamza's son and stepson and another man linked to the mosque. There was phone intercept evidence linking Hamza to the kidnappers and he was subsequently arrested by the British police. There was guarded optimism from the mosque trustees, who thought this might be the end of his iron grip, but he was released almost immediately by the authorities who were still hoping to use him as an informant.[5]

Hamza returned to the mosque and continued to preach his inflammatory sermons unimpeded. However, the kidnapping incident led to increased media attention and some highly critical coverage of his activities.

By this stage, the mosque was almost entirely under Hamza's control, despite the efforts of the trustees to moderate his influence. The British authorities may still have regarded him as a potentially useful but basically harmless buffoon, but the list of men exposed to his preaching whose names are now notorious suggests otherwise. Zacharias Moussaoui, convicted in connection with the 9/11 plot; Nizar Trabelsi, jailed for plotting a suicide attack on a Belgian NATO base; Shehzad Tanweer, Mohammed Sidique Khan and Jermaine Lindsey, three of the four suicide bombers who blew themselves up on London tube trains in the 7 July attacks of 2005; Richard Reid, the so-called 'shoe bomber' who had attempted to blow up an aircraft with explosives concealed in his shoes – all had passed through Finsbury Park Mosque at one time or another.

Concerns about Hamza and the mosque continued to grow. After the raid on Sidali Feddag's Wood Green flat in December 2002, the authorities finally decided to act. Among the findings at the flat had been the envelope that Kamel Bourgass had used to store over £4,000 in cash in the sports bag, and the poison recipes. Bourgass had made a crude attempt to disguise the address to which the envelope had originally been sent, but it wasn't difficult to decipher: 7–11, St Thomas's Road, London N4 2QH – the address for the Finsbury Park Mosque.

The subsequent police raid on the mosque revealed a cache of weapons and a stack of false identity documents, along with chequebooks and credit cards in false names. The finds could not be linked directly to Hamza himself, but a few weeks after the raid, in February 2003, he was suspended as a preacher by the Charity Commission, which ultimately regulates places of worship.

Undaunted, Hamza continued to preach to his numerous supporters in the street outside the mosque. His defiance and apparent immunity to legal sanctions continued to incense the British media. In an editorial, tabloid newspaper the *Sun*

wrote: 'Even with no hands, Hook [Hamza] raises two fingers
at the country he soils with his presence.'[6]

In 2004, Hamza was finally arrested for extradition
to the US to face charges of setting up a terror training
camp and providing support to Al-Qaeda. However, the
extradition process was stalled as the UK does not extradite in
circumstances where a defendant could face the death penalty.
In October 2004, Hamza was charged under British law with
various offences, including incitement to murder and intent
to incite racial hatred. He was convicted of eleven offences in
2006 and sentenced to a total of seven years' imprisonment.

The year following 9/11 saw two further major Al-Qaeda
attacks, with the bombing in October 2002 of a bar in Bali
and of a hotel in Kenya in November the same year. Al-Qaeda
clearly had both the determination and the capacity to carry
out atrocities around the world.

In such an understandably heightened atmosphere, it's no
surprise that the discoveries at the Wood Green flat were
seen as confirmation that the UK was next on the list for a
major terrorist outrage. Days after the police raid, the *Daily
Mail* reported: 'The discovery of the "kitchen sink" poison
factory in Wood Green is the first hard evidence of what
security officials have feared since 9/11 – that the UK is to
be the target for an attack by Osama bin Laden's Al-Qaeda
terror network.'[7]

Along with much of the rest of the UK media, the *Daily
Mail* was being fed a stream of information, formally and
informally, by Scotland Yard's anti-terror branch, linking the
Wood Green finds to a sophisticated international conspiracy.

The British press were certainly in good company
in swallowing this version of events unchallenged. On

5 February 2003, speaking to the United Nations Security Council, Colin Powell, then US Secretary of State, cited the supposed discovery of ricin at Wood Green as evidence of a 'sinister nexus' between Iraq and Al-Qaeda in an attempt to persuade the UN to support a war against Iraq.[8] The first attacks on Iraq soil came just six weeks later on 20 March – incidentally, the same day that UK government ministers were formally told that, contrary to earlier suggestions, no ricin had been found (a fact which wasn't made public until 2005).

Although the British and American authorities were keen to link the ricin find to Al-Qaeda and Iraq, some European security forces were much more sceptical. The French in particular dismissed claims of a link with Pakistan or Afghanistan, which would have been expected if there had been Al-Qaeda involvement. Instead, they believed the plot emanated from North Africa, an area that concerned the French far more, because of their historic colonial links in the region. They were also more dubious than the British about the reliability of the information being provided by Meguerba to the Algerians.

Indeed, for all Colin Powell's attempts to co-opt the ricin plot in support of the case for war and the alarming UK headlines, Bourgass's attempts at poison-making were more Blue Peter than Al-Qaeda. However murderous Bourgass and Meguerba's intentions, there was little real likelihood of their producing anything deadly from the poison recipes and ingredients they had assembled, let alone any realistic prospect of their using them to mount a wide-scale terror campaign.

So what had Meguerba and Bourgass been up to during their time in London? There is little independent evidence about their activities in the UK. Most of the information comes from Meguerba's testimony to the Algerians after his arrest and is, therefore, tainted. Meguerba was almost certainly subject to torture and had every incentive to tell his interrogators what he thought they wanted to hear. For their part, the Algerians had a vested interest in being seen to supply high-value information as proof of their good intentions and to cement their new relationship with Western governments.

Meguerba claimed that he and Bourgass had been trained as poison experts in terror camps in Afghanistan. When the pair met again in London in 2002, he says Bourgass had already put his training to good use and produced a quantity of ricin, which was stored in a Nivea face-cream pot. Bourgass, unsurprisingly, tells a different story, claiming in court that no ricin had ever been produced and the whole poison scheme had been Meguerba's idea, anyway.

It is unlikely that either man was being entirely truthful. What is known is that no ricin was ever found and the evidence recovered from the Wood Green flat undermines Meguerba's claim that the pair were highly trained in poison making. The items recovered reeked of amateurish dabblers, rather than hardened Al-Qaeda operatives. The prosecution claimed at trial that Bourgass was collecting cherry stones and apple pips to manufacture cyanide, but there are far easier ways of making the poison. Using that method, Bourgass would have needed a whole orchard, rather than the few plastic cupfuls of pips recovered.

Further, Meguerba told his interrogators that the plot included smearing 'ricin oil' on door handles in north London, apparently unaware that ricin isn't deadly if it's absorbed through the skin. Rather than being a master poisoner, Meguerba's comments suggest he had gleaned his information from reading the notes that Bourgass had written out, which mentioned mixing the ricin with cosmetic oil.

The prosecution tried to link the recipes to a 'Manual of Afghan Jihad' seized in 2000 and to two sets of notes found in Kabul in 2001. However, it seems more likely that Bourgass or Meguerba simply downloaded them from the internet – which would explain their lack of efficacy. The defence argued that the methodology of the recipes had more in common with instructions on a website run by an American survivalist called Kurt Saxon, who was notoriously anti-Muslim. Even Saxon's recipes are remarkably close to those contained in *The Poisoner's Handbook* by Maxwell Hutchkinson, a book available at the time of writing on Amazon for under £28.

However, there is little doubt about the malevolence of Bourgass and Meguerba's intentions. Indeed, Bourgass was soon to demonstrate his capacity to take human life with the brutal murder of a police officer; and he admitted in court that the plan was to use the poisons to kill (albeit in Algeria, rather than the UK).

But whatever their intentions, rather than ruthless profes-sionalism, Bourgass and Meguerba's activities were more notable for their amateurishness and incompetence. Even if the police had not discovered the plot, it is unlikely that planning by men who were little more than Al-Qaeda wannabees would have come to anything. However, in the heightened post-9/11 atmosphere, the finds at Wood Green were seen as evidence of an Al-Qaeda cell, poised to strike – and, through their loose links to the pair, the other defendants ended up being linked to an international terrorist conspiracy.

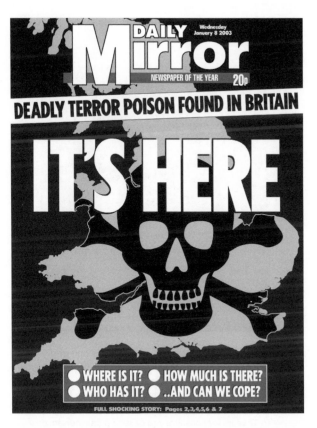

Figure 1 *Daily Mirror* front page, 8 January 2003, the day news of the Wood Green raid broke in the UK media. Despite the lurid headlines, which were typical of the press coverage that day, it was already clear to the authorities by this stage that no poison had been found at the flat. (Mirrorpix)

Figure 2   Kamel Bourgass was the only one of the five ricin defendants to be convicted. He has at least five known aliases and his true identity is unclear. Bourgass is currently serving a life sentence for the murder of DC Stephen Oake, and was also sentenced to 17 years for conspiracy to cause a public nuisance at the ricin trial. (Metropolitan Police handout/PA Archive/Press Association Images)

Figure 3 The shabby flat above a chemist shop in Wood Green, north London was labelled by the media the 'factory of death', following the police raid on 5 January 2003. Sidali Feddag had been allocated the accommodation after he applied for asylum. While Feddag subsequently house-sat for a family friend in East London, he allowed Kamel Bourgass to use the flat, with fateful consequences.

(Chris Young/PA Archive/Press Association Images)

Figure 4 The exterior of flats in Crumpsall Lane, Manchester. Police officers found Kamel Bourgass at this address, not knowing his identity. When they realised he was a wanted terror suspect, Bourgass was arrested. In his bid to escape he fatally stabbed DC Stephen Oake and wounded several other officers. (John Giles/PA Archive/Press Association Images)

Figure 5 A police officer places flowers outside the Crumpsall Lane property following the tragic death of Stephen Oake. (Martin Rickett/PA Archive/Press Association Images)

Figure 6 Abu Hamza al-Masri, the firebrand preacher associated with the Finsbury Park Mosque. Hamza was suspected by British police of recruiting for jihadi operations and was later convicted of soliciting murder and racial hatred, among other charges. He was sentenced to seven years' imprisonment in 2006.
(Johnny Green/PA Archive/Press Association Images)

Figure 7   Attendance at the Finsbury Park Mosque in north London was the common thread linking the five defendants. When it was raided in January 2003, police recovered a stun gun, blank firing pistols and various fraudulent chequebooks and false passports. Since the ricin trial, the mosque has sought to rebrand itself and is now called the North London Central Mosque, with a new board of trustees, new imams and a new ethos. (Lawrence Archer, March 2010)

Figure 8 The area around Blackstock Road is known as 'Little Algeria' because of its large number of Algerian-run shops and businesses. It is a stone's throw from the Finsbury Park Mosque and remains a magnet for the Algerian community in London. (Lawrence Archer, March 2010)

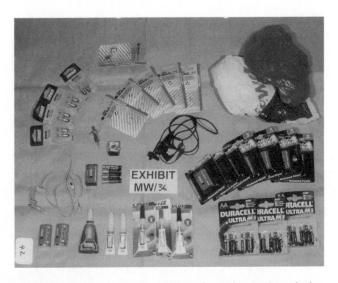

Figure 9   A Metropolitan Police handout photo, showing AA and other batteries, torch bulbs, superglue, a headset and various other items. After Kamel Bourgass's conviction for conspiracy, the *Daily Mirror* published this picture, with the caption: 'Electrical components. Enough kit to make several explosive devices.'(Metropolitan Police handout/PA Archive/ Press Association Images)

Figure 10 Items recovered from the Wood Green raid included 22 castor beans, stored in a pink jewellery box; a handful of cherry stones, found in the pan of a set of weighing scales; and a Nivea face-cream pot, containing a brown sludgy liquid. The prosecution claimed the beans and stones were for producing the poisons ricin and cyanide. The brown sludge may have been an unsuccessful attempt to make nicotine poison. However, at one stage, Sidali Feddag's brother came across the Nivea pot in the wardrobe and curious as to its contents stuck his finger in and gave it a sniff – to no obvious ill effect. (Metropolitan Police handout/ PA Archive/Press Association Images)

Figure 11 Acquitted defendant Mouloud Sihali had been described by the prosecution as the plot's 'Mr Fix-it', but jury foreman Lawrence Archer was later to give him another nickname: Encyclopedia Ricinica – because of Sihali's detailed knowledge about the case. Despite his acquittal, Sihali was rearrested in September 2005 and subjected to Draconian control order-like conditions for 19 months. He was finally cleared of being a threat to national security in May 2007 and was the subject of a flattering 21-page article in the American glossy magazine *Vanity Fair*. He is currently fighting deportation back to Algeria. (Lawrence Archer, 2008)

4
Mohammed Meguerba

Mohammed Meguerba was the ghost at the feast during the ricin trial. Although physically absent, having fled the UK in September 2002, his presence loomed large over the proceedings, with the prosecution portraying him as the shadowy and dangerous mastermind behind the plot.

Meguerba certainly played a pivotal role in the events that led to the ricin trial. Police were first led to Mouloud Sihali's flat after they found the Elgin Road address in Meguerba's possession when he was arrested in London in September 2002. Meguerba was subsequently released, but the raid on Elgin Road led to the arrests of Sihali and David Khalef. Meguerba's fingerprints were all over the poison recipes, and his former associate, Kamel Bourgass, insisted that all the suspect items at the Wood Green flat belonged to Meguerba. Further, it was Meguerba's company, Seven Roses, which the prosecution alleged was a front for money laundering.

What wasn't revealed in court was that Meguerba was also directly linked to the arrests of the other three defendants. Unknown to the jury, it was information that Meguerba gave to the Algerian secret police in December 2002 which had triggered the police raid on Sidali Feddag's flat at 352b High Road. After being questioned (and almost certainly tortured) by the notoriously brutal DRS, Meguerba provided a wealth of detail about his associates in the UK. It was this information which led directly to the raid on Feddag's Wood Green address and discovery of the so-called 'factory of death'.

Whereas little is known for certain about the other man at the heart of the plot, Kamel Bourgass (not even his real name), Meguerba's background is far less mysterious. The prosecution's portrayal of him as a calculating terrorist mastermind sits incongruously with some other known facts about Meguerba.

Meguerba was born in Algeria in 1968 and had lived in Dublin legitimately in the 1990s, where he'd had two disastrous marriages, including one to an Irish beautician who knew him as 'Frank'. Meguerba was the unlikely subject of a 'kiss and tell' exposé after the trial, when his beautician wife, Sharon Gray, sold her story to a Sunday tabloid ('My living hell as wife of top Al-Qaeda agent').[1] Gray, who married Meguerba in 1997, recounted how the 'fun-loving charmer' who had wooed her in a nightclub turned violent once they were married. Unsurprisingly, the marriage lasted just eight months.

It was in the aftermath of the break up of what was Meguerba's second marriage that he began to attend a mosque in Belfast. He subsequently told his Algerian interrogators that by early 2000, he had also starting going to an Islamic cultural centre, where he was first recruited to the cause of Al-Qaeda and radical Islam.

Meguerba had been picked up and interrogated by the Algerian police in December 2002. Ironically, given the brutal interrogation he almost certainly endured at the hands of the DRS, Meguerba had fled the UK to avoid being questioned by the British authorities. A few months before being picked up by the DRS, he had been arrested in London but after being released by the British authorities, he had decided to flee the country to avoid further questioning.

The interrogation techniques employed by the DRS are notorious for their brutality. There is evidence that Meguerba was tortured and, as is well recorded, testimony obtained under duress is notoriously unreliable. Meguerba's evidence is a fairly obvious ragbag of fact, exaggeration and distortion, mixed in with some complete fictions, invented to try to pacify his interrogators. For example, Meguerba described a training camp in Afghanistan in enough detail to suggest that he genuinely had been there, but also claimed to have personally met Osama bin Laden (who told him to keep up the good work). During questioning, Meguerba named virtually everyone he had ever met in London as collaborators in the plot.

The fact that Meguerba subsequently retracted much of his initial confession adds weight to the belief that it was obtained under duress. He later changed his story to insist his involvement in the plot was far less than he had originally said and, highly significantly, retracted his claim that one of the five defendants, Mustapha Taleb, was a mujahadeen associated with Algerian terror groups. By the time the case reached trial, Meguerba was claiming that he only knew Taleb from seeing him in the mosque bookshop where he worked, and that he didn't even know his name.

The techniques used by the DRS to persuade prisoners to make confessions are well documented. In 2006, Amnesty International published a report cataloguing some of them.[2] Methods included the 'chiffon', which involves forcing a cloth into the mouth of detainees to hold it open, so that dirty water or even chemicals can then be poured down their throats causing a sensation similar to drowning. Other methods included burning with cigarettes or soldering iron, throwing cigarette ash into detainees' eyes, whipping, slashing with sharp implements, and strangling almost to the point of suffocation. Amnesty also reported that the DRS has used electric torture, with shocks administered to the genitals and other sensitive parts of the body, sometimes after detainees were soaked with water to increase the intensity of shocks.

According to Amnesty, the DRS acts with almost complete impunity, with the civil authorities powerless to intervene and the judiciary routinely turning a blind eye to abuses.

It is impossible to know exactly what happened to Meguerba during questioning; however, another Algerian man with links to the ricin case gives a graphic first-hand account of DRS brutality. This man, who prefers to remain anonymous, was initially held in a police station but later blindfolded and moved to an unidentified location. There, he was put in a filthy cell, empty apart from a bucket to use as a lavatory. The cell walls were scrawled with messages from previous prisoners, written in the faint hope that these would get back to their families. There were bloodstains everywhere.

After being held for two or three days, the man was taken to a bigger room, where he was subjected to a 'good cop, bad cop' style of questioning. If he didn't give an identical answer to a repeated question, there were 'ramifications'. He was suspended by one wrist tied to a hook in the ceiling and his other wrist was attached to a heavy gas canister that dangled above the ground, not quite touching it. The pressure that being pulled apart in this way put on his chest and arms was excruciating and it was difficult to breathe. Eventually, his clavicle was dislocated, causing agonising pain. He passed out through lack of oxygen many times as he was kept in this position for hours on end.

This Algerian man reports that other prisoners were suspended by their wrists and ankles from a bar in the wall, in the 'gazelle' position, so called because the victim resembles a trussed animal brought back from a hunt. Some prisoners were tied to a chair and repeatedly pushed over to smash their heads on the ground. Some were sexually assaulted with bottles; others were beaten with iron bars or kicked in the back so hard as to make them lose consciousness. When they recovered, the process was repeated over and over again.

He claims that men were routinely held and tortured for indefinite periods and many died under interrogation. Their bodies, burned to disguise the marks of torture, were taken to towns at night and dumped with bullets in them, so that the authorities could blame anti-government 'terrorists' for the killings.

The DRS routinely used torture and there is evidence directly suggesting that Meguerba was brutalised during his time in custody. In May 2005, by which time he would have been held for 17 months, Meguerba's family claimed he had become a physical wreck, weighing just five and a half stone, looking frail and with missing teeth.[3] A man who was held with him says Meguerba had skin missing from his face and a badly dislocated shoulder.

Such claims are all but impossible to verify, but what is known is that a few days after being picked up by the DRS in December 2002, Meguerba was providing his captors with a wealth of information about his supposed activities and associates in the UK.

Meguerba told the DRS he had been sent by his Al-Qaeda masters for terrorist training in summer 2000, after travelling from Ireland to London. He claimed to have been given a false French passport and sent to Afghanistan via Pakistan in early 2001 to be trained in armaments, poisons and explosives. He then claimed to have left Afghanistan a few weeks before the 9/11 attacks on New York, to prepare for the expected American backlash against the impending atrocity.

In any event, in August 2001, Meguerba turned up at Schipol airport in Holland after flying in from Tehran, Iran. He was detained by the Dutch authorities because of inconsistencies in his passport (which was, in fact, false) and was kept under arrest for six months, during which time he applied for asylum five times. He was twice taken to the Algerian embassy for repatriation, but refused to return home and was eventually released in February 2002. Travelling to France, Meguerba was immediately granted a new passport at the Algerian embassy in Paris. By March 2002 he had arrived in London.

If Meguerba was a religious extremist at this stage, acting under instruction from Al-Qaeda, he showed little outward sign of it. His associates remember him as a nervous character, who had embraced Western dress and Western ways: clean shaven, drinking alcohol and praying irregularly. Mouloud Sihali, who resented having Meguerba foisted on him as a room-mate, had little respect for him, regarding him as a freeloader, who abused other people's hospitality. Far from being a sinister, brooding figure, Meguerba was a chatterbox, known for talking non-stop. He was never without his mobile phone – so much so, that Sihali describes Meguerba's phone as being 'like his girlfriend'.

In fact, unknown to Sihali, Meguerba had a real girlfriend who he was planning to marry and install in Sihali's Ilford flat. All Algerian men face strong cultural pressure to marry and Meguerba, who was by now in his late thirties, was no exception. Despite his two short-lived marriages – with his first (to Katrina Herbert) ending after two months on grounds of 'incompatibility'; the other, after eight months when Sharon Gray took out a restraining order against him – Meguerba had become engaged to a Moroccan woman, whom he intended to bring to London.

In August, the brooding dislike between Sihali and Meguerba burst into the open when Sihali was warned by a mutual acquaintance that Meguerba planned to move his fiancée into Elgin Road. Sihali reacted with fury. He had acquired the flat specifically as a home for his own intended bride – whom he planned to bring over from France in September or October – and had only allowed Meguerba to stay there to keep the peace with other tenants at David Khalef's flat. He promptly ordered Meguerba out of Elgin Road and Meguerba had little option other than to comply. Crucially, he left behind some of his property in the flat for the police to discover later.

Like so many of his countrymen, Meguerba had gravitated towards the Finsbury Park area and its mosque during his time in London. It was here that he first met Omar Djedid, who subsequently became his friend and business partner. It is unclear whether Meguerba knew Djedid had recently escaped from immigration detention but, other than being concerned at the unwanted attention from the authorities that such an association might bring to him, it seems unlikely that Meguerba would have been too concerned. Djedid was certainly useful to Meguerba. He introduced Meguerba to David Khalef, and persuaded Khalef to allow the pair to say at his room at 240 High Road, Ilford (much to the annoyance of Khalef's existing room-mate, Sihali). And it was Djedid who subsequently asked Sihali if he would be company secretary to Meguerba's Seven Roses business venture (which Sihali agreed to do as a favour to Djedid, despite his dislike of Meguerba).

Mohammed Meguerba had contact with other Algerians while he was in the UK, too. These included a wiry, intense young Algerian called Kamel Bourgass (known to Meguerba as Nadir) and Khaled Alwerfeli, who owned the flat in Manchester where Bourgass would later fatally stab DC Stephen Oake during his arrest. According to Meguerba's 'confession' to the DRS, he and Bourgass had first met at terror training camps in Afghanistan, where they had both been handpicked to be 'chemists', tutored in the art of poison making.

However, even while Meguerba was busy plotting, it seems his terrorist activities were only one string to his bow. He continued with his other business venture, setting up his confectionary company, Seven Roses, in order to secure better sites at the various markets where the sweets were sold. Rather than keeping as low a profile as possible Meguerba continued with activities which risked bringing him to the attention of the authorities.

Whatever Meguerba's true intentions during his time in the UK, the British had missed an opportunity to hold him weeks before he fled to Algeria. On 18 September 2002, Meguerba had been picked up by the British anti-terror police after a raid on an address in Tottenham.

It was not the first time Meguerba had come to the attention of the UK police. In summer 2002, he was arrested in Norwich for cheque fraud, but had subsequently been released on bail. When Meguerba was arrested again in September, he was taken to the high-security police station at Paddington Green in west London for questioning. Once there, he claimed to be in the UK legitimately and offered to prove the fact by producing his marriage certificate, which showed he was married to an Irish woman.

While in custody, Meguerba suffered what appeared to be an epileptic fit and was taken to hospital for treatment. He had a history of epilepsy, which was apparently a legacy of being hit on the head with a weapon during his National Service in Algeria. Although Meguerba was originally arrested on suspicion of being 'concerned in funding of proscribed organisations', at this stage, he was clearly not on the British police's radar as a serious threat. He was later de-arrested on the funding charges and then promptly re-arrested for possession of a false passport, deception and illegal entry to the UK. He was given bail and ordered to report back to the police on 11 December, some three months later.

During questioning, police found a piece of paper in Meguerba's wallet with the address for Mouloud Sihali's flat at 103d Elgin Road, Ilford. Although they were sufficiently unconcerned about Meguerba to release him on bail, police were curious enough about his associates to put Elgin Road under surveillance. Eventually, they spotted someone they were interested in, the man who had previously escaped from immigration detention, Omar Djedid.

On 19 September 2002, police raided the Elgin Road flat, where they arrested Djedid and discovered Meguerba's passport and the other documents he'd left behind when Sihali threw him out a few weeks earlier. As the leaseholder of the flat (albeit in a false name), Sihali also came under suspicion and was taken in for questioning. For the first time, Sihali learned that the real name of the man he had known only as Sofiane was Mohammed Meguerba. Unaware of the seriousness of the investigation, Sihali gave police David Khalef's address at 240 High Road, where police went on to discover a stash of false passports. From there, they rapidly tracked Khalef down to his Norfolk address. Once again, police recovered false identity documents but also something potentially more incriminating: tucked into a suitcase belonging to Khalef was a photocopy of a handwritten recipe for making ricin and other potentially deadly poisons.

Meguerba was, however, oblivious to the sequence of events that his arrest had set in train. After his release on bail in September, rather than risk further trouble from the British authorities, he had fled London. He headed initially for Manchester and then flew out from John Lennon airport in Liverpool – where security was more relaxed than at London airports – on a false French passport. He travelled through Spain and eventually arrived in Morocco, where he stayed with his fiancée, whose father was a local tribal chief and allegedly an Al-Qaeda supporter.

From Morocco, Meguerba somehow found his way to Algeria, where he joined a group of fighters. It seems likely he may have been smuggled into Algeria by a people trafficker from Marrakech but, however he got there, it was to be a fateful move. On 16 December, he was picked up by the security services in Algeria and held in custody until 28 December, when his interrogation began.

Once in custody, Meguerba either rapidly decided to be exceptionally cooperative, or the Algerians employed highly effective interrogation methods. (In court, Bourgass claimed that Meguerba was, in fact, working for the Algerians as an agent provocateur, based largely on the fact that he made a number of phone calls while in custody, one of which was to Britain to incite further action on the ricin plot.)

Meguerba provided the Algerians with a detailed account of his conversion to Islamic radicalism and his training at the terror camps, including the specifics of stripping and cleaning various weapons, such as Uzis and Kalashnikovs. Along with details of his movements, he gave the names of dozens of associates in London. These included one known as 'Nadir' (Kamel Bourgass), who Meguerba claimed was planning an imminent poison attack. Meguerba reported having seen at first hand Bourgass's attempts at making various poisons, including the successful production of ricin, which he'd seen being stored in a Nivea face-cream jar.

Meguerba claimed that a man called Rabah Kadre (who also went by the name Toufiq) was the local captain of the terror cell and had provided £4,000 for Meguerba to set up Seven Roses. Kadre was also alleged to be responsible for scouting and choosing possible targets for the ricin that 'Nadir' – or Bourgass – was manufacturing. The plan was for the poison to be smeared on car door handles, Meguerba being adamant (entirely wrongly) that the 'ricin oil' could be easily absorbed through the skin. Meguerba provided a mobile number for Bourgass and an address where he said the poisons were being made: 12 Harrow Road, Wood Green.

On 31 December the British intelligence services received a chilling warning from the Algerians: *'The group of Algerian terrorists in London have a quantity of fatal poison (of the family of toxic products which act through the skin) which they intend to use in the next few days.'*

The British had been in a state of high alert following the 9/11 terrorist attacks on America and took the warning seriously. However, they rapidly discovered that the information supplied by the Algerians was flawed: the mobile number didn't work and there was no such address as 12 Harrow Road in Wood Green.

The Algerians continued to question Meguerba. By 2 January, the British police had a detailed description of the location of the property where the poisons were being made – which they were able to identify as Feddag's shabby flat above a pharmacy in Wood Green.

Three days later, on 5 January 2003, police stormed into the one-bedroom flat at 352b High Road. 'Nadir' was nowhere to be found – Bourgass having previously moved out – but he had left behind evidence of his illicit activities. Items seized by police included over £4,000 in cash, copies of the poison recipes, various chemicals, latex gloves, thermometers, and electronic scales for measuring small weights. On the face of it, the police had found their poison factory. When initial tests on a pestle and mortar indicated the possibility of ricin, it seemed to confirm that they had uncovered a major terrorist conspiracy. Feddag and, later, Mustapha Taleb, who had worked the photocopier at Finsbury Park Mosque, were both arrested.

On 8 January 2003, news of the ricin plot hit the national media, with newspaper headlines announcing that a sophisticated plot to poison the British public had been broken by police. At this point, the man at the heart of the conspiracy, Kamel Bourgass, was still at liberty as he was no longer living at 352b when it was raided, having moved out in late 2002 to make room for Feddag's brother. When Bourgass saw the media coverage about the finds at his old address, he fled to Manchester. It was here, six days later, that the police stumbled across him when they went to arrest another man – which was to have fatal consequences for DC Stephen Oake.

Mouloud Sihali and David Khalef were still in custody and could now be linked, police believed, to the Wood Green 'factory of death' by the poison recipes found in Khalef's suitcase. It was Meguerba who had triggered the pair's arrest after police found Sihali's address in his wallet in September. Now his confessions had led police to Bourgass and also Feddag and Taleb. Wittingly or otherwise, from his cell in Algeria, he had supplied the missing piece of the jigsaw. Based on the evidence from Meguerba's 'confessions' and the suspect items recovered during raids in Norfolk, Ilford and Wood Green, the British authorities were now convinced they had uncovered a major terrorist conspiracy.

Although Meguerba's confessions were central to the prosecution case, they were never admitted in the court proceedings. Even leaving aside the question of whether they had been obtained by coercion, they fell well short of the standards of evidence required by British courts. The confessions were not provided as a verbatim report of his interrogation, but in the form of a bullet point summary; it was not a direct and approved translation of the original Arabic into English; and Meguerba had had no legal representation during his questioning.

By the time the case was heading for trial, there were further problems as, by then, Meguerba had retracted large parts of his evidence. In October 2003, after months of negotiation, British anti-terror police went to Algeria to interview Meguerba for themselves. The interview was conducted under a process known as Commission Rogatoire, which required questions to be submitted in writing in advance. The interview was not a great success for the police, who were hoping Meguerba would help bolster the prosecution case. They found him far less cooperative than he had apparently been when first questioned by the Algerians. He flatly refused to answer anything that hadn't been submitted in writing and decided not to talk about certain things that had happened in Afghanistan, Ireland and England. 'There are some questions that I answer and some other [sic] I don't answer', he told his British interrogators.

The defence legal teams had even less success with Meguerba than the prosecution. Lawyers for Mouloud Sihali and Sidali Feddag (neither of whom had been named in Meguerba's evidence) made numerous attempts to interview him in the hope this would exonerate their clients, but their requests were consistently refused.

5

Arrests

The police inquiry which led to the ricin arrests was known as Operation Springbourne, launched in 2002 by SO13, the anti-terror branch of the British police, in the wake of the 9/11 attacks on America. The operation was a huge undertaking, lasting three years and spanning 26 other jurisdictions as well as the UK. One of its aims was to try to weaken Al-Qaeda by tracing and cutting off funding for its terrorist activities which was emanating from the UK.

During its investigations, Operation Springbourne uncovered a crude but effective fraud to raise funds, where goods would be bought from shops using forged or stolen chequebooks or credit cards. The items would then be returned for a refund before the retailer discovered the payment was false and any cash raised would be sent out of the country to fund Al-Qaeda activities in North Africa and Pakistan.

On 18 September 2002, as part of its investigation into these financial scams, police went to an address in Tottenham to arrest a man on suspicion of fraud. Purely by chance, Mohammed Meguerba was at the property when police arrived and was also taken in for questioning.

Despite the seriousness of the inquiry, Meguerba was given bail and told to report back to police in three months' time.

Instead, he fled, eventually ending up back in Algeria, but the address found in his wallet was to lead police to Sihali's newly acquired flat at 103d Elgin Road.

On the 19 September, unaware that he was being watched, Omar Djedid left the Elgin Road flat and met up with his room-mate, Sihali. Djedid was still sleeping at 103d regularly and, after Meguerba's departure a few weeks earlier, relations between the pair were amicable. They had a series of errands to run – Djedid went for a shave and to have his photo taken for a travel pass – before going to the nearby Talk & Surf internet café. Djedid wanted Sihali's help with making an online application for a £15,000 bank loan to buy a van. Sihali, with his intelligence and good language skills, was well known in the community as someone who could help with this kind of task. Djedid's English was poor and his computer skills were not good, so under his instructions Sihali entered information on the bank's website.

The pair had been working on the application for a while when they were approached by two police officers from SO13. The officers were in plain clothes but claimed in their subsequent witness statements that they had clearly identified themselves as being from the anti-terror police. Sihali, however, tells a different story. He insists that he and Djedid were told they were being questioned over a minor immigration matter. Sihali was unaware that Djedid had earlier escaped from immigration detention but, for anyone living under the radar as he was, avoiding the attentions of the immigration authorities was an occupational hazard. He told the officials he was Omar Nait Atmane, the name that appeared on his doctored French passport, and was not unduly concerned about what might happen.

At this stage, it was Djedid who was the focus of the police attention. They took him aside for questioning while Sihali remained seated. After a few minutes, something he said sparked their interest in his companion and one of the men returned to talk to Sihali. Why, the officer wanted to know, had Djedid told them Sihali's name was 'Mujad', while Sihali himself had said he was called Omar?

It was a seemingly minor slip – and one which, if the men really had been planning a major terrorist outrage, they would have been careful to avoid. In the hours of questioning and months of incarceration that followed, Sihali must have reflected on the fact that, if only he and Djedid had got their story straight about what name he was using, he might have avoided the police's attention all together.

As it was, the discrepancy was enough for both men to be arrested on suspicion of entering the country illegally and to be taken away for further questioning. Sihali, however, remained hopeful that the ruse of his cousin's doctored passport would hold and was confident enough to tell the police to go ahead and check up on him as they wouldn't find anything untoward.

Sihali was taken first to a police station in nearby Ilford and then transferred to one in Barking. It was several hours before he was questioned. Again, he told police his name was Omar Nait Atmane. He claimed to be French and gave his address as 103d Elgin Road, Ilford. When questioned further, he said he had previously been living at a house nearby – David Khalef's flat at 240 High Road. Djedid had the keys for Elgin Road (as he had been the last one to leave the flat that day), but Sihali voluntarily handed the police the keys for Khalef's property that were in his keeping.

His police interview went on for many hours but Sihali did not exercise his right to have a solicitor present. Throughout this period, he still believed it was an immigration matter and that his safest option was to stick to his story of being Omar Nait Atmane.

However, as the questioning continued into the early hours, Sihali began to realise that he might be in more trouble than he had thought. By the middle of the night, Sihali was fearful enough to ask to phone a solicitor. The solicitor quickly realised from Sihali's description that these were not immigration officers and advised him to say nothing until he had a lawyer present. Although Sihali was beginning to understand the seriousness of his situation, he was still hoping it would blow over and that he would soon be released. At one point it looked as if his strategy might pay off, as when police checked the name Omar Nait Atmane with the French Embassy, just as Sihali had hoped, it came back clean. But still the police did not release him.

Sihali remained in custody overnight but the following day the police's attitude towards him seemed to have softened. One of the officers apologised for the delay in releasing him and asked for a favour: could Sihali let them look at both the Elgin Road and High Road properties? After hours of intense questioning, Sihali was struck by the politeness of the officer's request and, assuming that if he cooperated he would be released more quickly, he was happy to comply.

Sihali was taken by police to each flat in turn and answered their questions about who owned which items. Later in the afternoon, Sihali was taken back to the police station, cautioned for deception in relation to Djedid's bank loan and told he could go. The police had just one further request: would he agree to keep away from both 103d and 240 until officers had had the chance to take another look at each property? Still anxious to be cooperative, Sihali agreed not to go back to either address.

After being held for many hours and subject to prolonged questioning, Sihali's relief at being released without his illegal immigration status being discovered was palpable. It had been a deeply unpleasant and unsettling experience, but he had cooperated with police and, crucially, his false identity as Omar Nait Atmane had remained intact. The keys to Khalef's flat, which had been in Sihali's possession when he was arrested, were returned to him. However, the police wouldn't give him the keys to his own flat at Elgin Road as these had been found on Djedid and would, therefore, have to be returned to Djedid.

For someone who was to be portrayed by the prosecution as the Mr Fix-it for a terrorist cell, Sihali seems to have been remarkably compliant. After being released from police custody, rather than fleeing immediately (as Meguerba had done) or going straight to Elgin Road to destroy any incriminating evidence, Sihali wandered the streets until late evening. Eventually, he cadged a bed for the night from a friend in the nearby north London area of Manor House. His actions in meekly complying with the police request to stay away from both properties suggest that at this stage he still had no idea that he was about to be linked with a terrorist plot.

In the morning, Sihali went back to 240 High Road, where he was soon found by the police sitting at the kitchen table. Asked why he was there, he said he come to check if there was any mail. As before, Sihali was cooperative and showed the officers Khalef's room, after retrieving the room key from its hiding place under the doormat.

Officers had been into the room the day before, but this time they did a more thorough search. Hidden in the base of one of the beds they found a padded envelope containing the stash of stolen and doctored passports, along with some blank, fake ID cards. Sihali was promptly arrested for 'being concerned in the funding and instigating of terrorism' and taken to the high-security police station at Paddington Green. Only then did Sihali realise that he was in serious trouble.

British interrogation techniques are mild compared with those used by police in Sihali's native Algeria, but he was still to find the experience of being repeatedly questioned over the next nine days highly traumatic. Sihali says he felt 'like an insect in a jar'[1] and began to hallucinate, imagining he could hear voices calling his name. He was held alone in a small cell, with one window high up in the wall. Sihali believes the harsh conditions were designed to dehumanise him and try to break his spirit. The light was never turned off and he was checked on regularly: each time, the officer would slam the spy hole shut noisily, which meant Sihali couldn't get any proper sleep. His own clothing was taken away and he was given clothes to wear which irritated his skin. He was nearly driven mad by being asked the same questions over and over again. For three days, he wasn't allowed to wash or shave or comb his hair. His skin turned grey. He says: 'They came to take a picture of me to confirm with my family who I was. When my brother saw the photo he hardly recognised me. He said I looked like a tramp, a wolf-man!'[2]

Despite this, Sihali continued to try to be cooperative, confirming that the room at 240 belonged to David Khalef and providing an address for Khalef in Norfolk. Even now, he stuck to his story of being a French citizen called Omar Nait Atmane – the name under which he had leased the flat at

Elgin Road. Sihali was too frightened of making things worse to confess to having used a false name and still clung to the hope he might be released if he stuck to his original story.

During a search of Elgin Road, police had recovered property belonging to the absent Mohammed Meguerba and to Omar Djedid – who was still being questioned. At 240 High Road, they found some of Sihali's personal papers, including two false passports bearing his photograph, plus his Algerian identity card giving his real name. Faced with this evidence, Sihali now had little choice but to admit he had lied repeatedly about his real identity and that he had entered the country illegally. Meanwhile, the information he had supplied about David Khalef was being followed up. On 26 September, a detective sergeant from SO13 who was in Norfolk on other business was sent to the address for Khalef that Sihali had provided. This turned out to be out of date, but the detective was directed to the correct one: 9 Ethel Coleman Way, Thetford, a three-bedroom rented house on a modern estate. Khalef had been staying there while he worked at various local meat factories, doing jobs such as gutting and preparing chickens, packing and loading.

Police subsequently arrived at Ethel Coleman Way, armed with a search warrant. Initially, they knocked on the front door but, when they got no reply, smashed it down and raced up the stairs to find David Khalef, still in bed. Khalef was duly cautioned under the Terrorism Act and asked if he spoke English, to which he replied: 'Yes, but I am not a terrorist.'

Khalef's accommodation in Thetford was fairly basic. The room contained two single beds (he shared the room with a Portuguese man), a smattering of furniture, some cannabis leaves (which Khalef claimed were his room-mate's), clothing and other possessions. Among Khalef's belongings was a soft zipped bag with a collapsible handle for pulling it along: hidden inside the space that the handle folded into, police discovered a folded sheet of birthday wrapping paper. Inside the paper were a passport bearing Khalef's picture, an Italian driving licence also with his picture but bearing the name Dominico Esposito, and several photocopied sheets of paper. Among the writing on the photocopies appeared to be a chemical formula written largely in Arabic. However, interspersed with the Arabic script were English words which needed no translation: 'cyanide' and 'ricin'. The police had found the first in what would turn out to be several copies of the poison recipes written out by Kamel Bourgass, which were at the heart of the ricin trial.

David Khalef was initially taken to a local police station before being transferred to Paddington Green, where Sihali and Djedid were still being held. Like them, he was questioned over many days – a process that the childlike Khalef found both bewildering and distressing.

On translation, the photocopies found in Khalef's bag were shown to be recipes for making various poisons from simple and widely available ingredients. These poisons included cyanide, but also what were described as 'potato poison' (solanine), 'tobacco poison' (nicotine), 'rotten meat poison' (botulinum), and 'castor bean poison' (ricin). There were instructions for making crude but potentially lethal explosives, also from easily obtainable materials, such as agricultural fertiliser; and a diagram for what was subsequently shown to be an electronic detonator. There was also a separate list of chemicals, which appeared to be photocopied from a textbook, showing their household names, common uses and where they could be obtained. A number of the chemicals on this list were ingredients in the poison recipes.

Khalef has never convincingly explained how he came by the recipes. His account during police questioning was hardly plausible: he claimed to have been given them to 'look after' by a man named Ali, and that he knew nothing else about them. His fingerprints were found on the pages, showing he must have handled them, but as he was barely literate, Khalef would have understood little of what was written on them.

Mouloud Sihali was also questioned extensively about the poison recipes. His English and reading skills were far superior to Khalef's and he managed to translate some of the text from Arabic into English, but many words were technical terms that he did not know and it was apparent he had never seen the photocopies before. There was no fingerprint evidence to indicate that Sihali had ever handled the recipes, so it seemed that whoever had given them to Khalef, it wasn't him. Neither man had any idea who had written the original documents from which the photocopies were made, nor of their ultimate purpose.

The recipes, taken together with the stash of false passports found in the bed base at 240 High Road, on which both men's fingerprints were found, was enough to convince police they were dealing with a terrorist conspiracy. In September 2002, both Mouloud Sihali and David Khalef were charged under the Terrorism Act and held in custody at Belmarsh prison awaiting trial.

On 17 November, the day before they were due to make a court appearance, the *Sunday Times*[3] reported that the men were 'part of a gang of suspected Al-Qaeda terrorists' who planned to 'kill commuters on the London Underground by releasing poison gas in a crowded carriage'. Another broadsheet, the *Independent on Sunday*, claimed they were plotting to plant a dirty bomb on a 'ferry using a British port'.⁴ There were other reports of a plot to release cyanide gas. It's unclear where these lurid stories came from (even the then Home Secretary David Blunkett described reports of a planned gas attack as 'nonsense') and, in fact, the Algerians were facing charges of possessing fake identity documents, for terrorist purposes.

Among Omar Djedid's possessions, police had also found fake identity documents, along with items they believed were linked to Islamic extremism. There was nothing, however, to tie him directly to the poison recipes, so he continued to be held on immigration grounds. Although central to the chain of events that led to the ricin trial, Djedid was never charged with any terrorist offences and, in 2007, while still in detention, agreed to return voluntarily to Algeria.

The charges against Sihali and Khalef were an apparent success for Operation Springbourne, but it was clear that key pieces of the jigsaw were missing. Police didn't know who had written out the recipes in the first place, nor the extent of the conspiracy. Crucially, they had no idea whether any poisons or explosives had been made, nor where or when they were intended to be used.

It was a puzzle which was apparently resolved in dramatic fashion with the receipt on 31 December 2002 of the stark message from the Algerian secret police warning of a poison attack planned to happen in the next few days. According to the confession made by Meguerba to the Algerians, not only had the plotters managed to make poisons but they were about to unleash them in the British capital.

The UK anti-terror police moved quickly. From information provided by Meguerba, they identified Feddag's shabby flat in Wood Green as the makeshift laboratory where the poisons were being made. Meguerba's co-conspirator 'Nadir' – also known as Kamel Bourgass – had been living at the address but, unbeknown to Meguerba in his cell in Algeria, had moved out days earlier. By the end of 2002, 352b High Road was being used by Sidali Feddag's two brothers, Mouloud and Samir. Sidali Feddag himself was rarely there. He was house-sitting in Leyton, east London, for the family friend who had gone abroad and didn't want to leave his flat empty, following a burglary at the flat downstairs.

Police put the 352b address under surveillance. It seems likely that they followed Mouloud Feddag from Wood Green when he went to visit his brother Sidali in Leyton on 4 January, where he stayed the night.

At about 6 a.m. on the 5 January 2003, in what was a coordinated anti-terror operation, police arrived at the Leyton flat. Sidali Feddag, who had been up until 4 a.m. watching videos, was woken by police hammering on the front door. In his sleepy state, Feddag's initial assumption was that the police presence was something to do with the recent break-in downstairs. He opened the door and was asked whether he was the tenant of the Wood Green flat. Feddag confirmed he was, and was promptly arrested. He and his brother, Mouloud, were then taken away for questioning.

At around the same time, police were mounting a similar raid on what they believed was the terror cell's poison factory at 352b High Road. The officers at Wood Green were accompanied by scientists from the government's Defence Science and Technology Laboratory, based at Porton Down. All were wearing protective clothing and face masks in the expectation of finding highly toxic materials.

Officers burst into the flat to find the third Feddag brother, Samir, groggy, confused and probably still drunk from the night before – but no sign of their main target, Bourgass.

Feddag's flat in Wood Green had been provided for him by the local authority. The accommodation was basic and cramped: it had a living room, which was used as a bedroom by another man who was never linked to the plot; a communal kitchen and bathroom; and a double bedroom, where Samir Feddag had been sleeping. The room had no bed, just a mattress on the floor, and a few items of furniture. Unsurprisingly, given the number of people who were staying there, the room was untidy, with various sports bags and carrier bags scattered over the floor.

Many of the items recovered by police were the kind of detritus you would expect to find in a room used by a group of single men, living a transient lifestyle – clothing, toiletries, household goods. However, they also found a locked sports bag containing over £4,000. The money was kept in the envelope from the immigration office which had previously notified Bourgass that his asylum claim – made in the name of Nadir Habra – had failed.

Equally of interest to police, the bag contained what turned out to be the original version of the recipes that had been found in Khalef's Thetford room three months earlier. There was also a smaller version of the recipes, which had been folded up many times to make it small enough to hide easily. There was another photocopy of the original recipe in a drawer at the base of the wardrobe.

On the top of the wardrobe police found a set of domestic weighing scales, the pan of which contained cherry stones, one of the ingredients for cyanide listed in the recipes; down the side of the wardrobe was a polystyrene cup containing apple pips, another ingredient for making cyanide. In the chest of drawers, inside a small pink jewellery box, were 22 pink and black striped castor beans, an ingredient for making ricin. In the bottom compartment of the wardrobe were three plastic bottles, one containing isopropanol (rubbing alcohol), the other two holding acetone (the main ingredient of nail varnish remover) – substances which were both listed as ingredients in the poison recipes. There were also jars containing various herbs and spices and honey.

There were various other potentially incriminating items: latex medical gloves; heavier domestic rubber gloves; various thermometers; a hand-operated coffee mill and a marble pestle and mortar, either of which could be used for grinding the poison ingredients. There was a set of electronic scales for accurately measuring tiny quantities; blotting paper and a funnel, that could have been used for filtering poisons.

In another compartment in the wardrobe was a Nivea face-cream jar containing a brown sludge, which turned out to be a mixture of nicotine and isopropanol. If this was the result of an attempt to make 'tobacco poison', it was as crude as it was unsuccessful: one of Feddag's brothers had previously stumbled across the jar in the wardrobe and, curious as to what it contained, had stuck his finger into the contents and given it a good sniff, to no obvious ill effect.

The chief scientist from Porton Down did a series of 'presumptive tests' at the scene to see if there was any evidence of toxins being present. Most items tested came back negative – no evidence of poison. However, the initial result for the pestle and mortar indicated the possibility of ricin. The scientist would need to conduct a series of more rigorous tests back at the laboratory before the presence of ricin could be confirmed, but this finding, taken with discovery of the recipes and the small stash of castor beans, seemed to point to the police having broken up a terrorist cell on the brink of a poisoning campaign.

After his arrest in Leyton and the raid on his Wood Green flat, Sidali Feddag was questioned extensively by police. Feddag, who spoke reasonable English, was initially asked about his background and associates, and how he spent his time. Gradually, the questioning came round to items found in the Wood Green flat. Feddag was asked to translate the Arabic writing on the photocopied recipes. He stumbled over the exact meanings of some words, although could give the gist of them, saying for instance 'acid of liquid of lemon' instead of 'acetic acid'. When he spotted the references in the recipes to apple seeds and cherry stones, he volunteered the fact that he had some of these in his flat.

Feddag had little idea of what he was suspected of doing and was shocked when police revealed they had found poison recipes in his flat. His reaction was a mixture of puzzlement and horror, exclaiming: 'You mean there are chemical weapons in my flat!'

Feddag was now thrown into panic and desperate to convince police that the apparently suspect items were not his, but had been left behind by his former flatmate, 'Nadir' (the name Bourgass was using). For a while, police appeared to think Feddag had invented Nadir as a way of shifting the blame away from himself. Eventually, they were convinced of his existence, when Feddag showed them Nadir's mobile-phone number in his own phone's memory and after finding a photo of a man matching Feddag's description of 'Nadir' in the wardrobe at the flat.

Feddag had met Bourgass (or Nadir) via the mosque in spring 2002 and let him stay at the flat for around nine months. He knew the habitual shoplifter Nadir was a petty criminal but refused to believe he was guilty of anything as serious as a terrorist plot. Feddag insisted to police that the items they saw as evidence of a poison plot were entirely innocent. The fruit seeds and castor beans were for making traditional Arabic herbal remedies, he said. Nadir would crack open the cherry stones that Feddag had agreed to save and use the pulp to make a drink to ease a stomach complaint. Similarly, Feddag's father had agreed to bring over castor beans from Algeria at Nadir's request as these, too, were used in homemade medicines. The coffee grinder and pestle and mortar were for grinding up seeds and pips, to make remedies that Nadir's grandmother had taught him to make.

If Feddag genuinely saw nothing sinister in Bourgass's accumulated belongings, his naivety may have been at least in part down to his age. He was just 17 when he was arrested, having come to the UK as a 15 year old. The experience of leaving his family behind so young had given Feddag a degree of maturity beyond his years – yet there were times when it was clear that his level of understanding was still that of a child: for example, he described Nadir (who was in his late twenties or early thirties) to police as 'old'.

The one question Feddag could not answer was where his former flatmate was currently to be found. Police sent a bulletin to all national police forces to track him down, but to no avail. Since he had stopped sleeping at Feddag's flat, no one knew where Bourgass had gone.

Although police had failed to find their chief suspect, other aspects of their investigations were continuing. The pestle and mortar which had shown an initial positive result for ricin was taken to the laboratory at Porton Down for further analysis. Over the next two days, scientists ran a battery of tests which all came back negative. By 7 January (two days after the raid), it had been established that no ricin had been found, after all.

Despite this, the story leaked to the media was the exact opposite. Rather than seeking to reassure the public that there was no evidence of any poisons having been made, on 8 January the national press was full of stories about the 'ricin plot' and the Wood Green 'factory of death'. Even the prime minister Tony Blair waded in, telling the media the arrests of the men showed, 'this danger is present and real, and with us now...'.[5]

Apart from stoking public fear, the other consequence of the extensive media coverage was to alert Bourgass to the fact police would be looking for him and prompt him to flee London. Ironically, it was the release of this false information about the ricin find that prompted the chief suspect in the case to flee. Bourgass subsequently landed up in Manchester where, seven days later, police would stumble across him when they went to a house to arrest a suspect in another terrorist case. It was as Bourgass tried to escape that he stabbed DC Stephen Oake to death and wounded three of his colleagues.

It has never been clarified how this wrong information, the release of which was to have deadly consequences, reached the media.

Following the capture of Bourgass, police steadily rounded up more and more suspects with links to him or Meguerba or the various men already detained in prison. Soon, there were over 100 people brought in for questioning. A pattern began to emerge: many of the suspects had links to the Finsbury Park Mosque and its local community. Among those with direct links to the mosque named by Meguerba as fellow plotters were the bookshop owner, Nasreddine Fekhadji, and his assistant, Mustapha Taleb.

Fekhadji was arrested on 5 January and charged as a member of the ricin plot. However, Fekhadji's mental health was clearly extremely fragile and the charges against him were eventually dropped. Instead, police turned their attention to Taleb, who helped him run the shop.

Taleb was approached by officers on 7 January, as he was about to pay money into a bank in Wood Green. Alone among the ricin defendants, Taleb was in the UK legally (having won an asylum appeal in 2000), but he was not surprised to be picked up by police as he had heard about Fekhadji's arrest two day's earlier. What Taleb didn't know at this stage was that he was being linked to the ricin plot as his fingerprint had been found on the back of one of the poison recipes.

The mosque had long been notorious because of its association with the radical preacher Abu Hamza, but it now appeared to be at the heart of the unfolding conspiracy. A decision was taken to raid the mosque to seek more evidence relating to the plot. On 19 January 2002, Operation Mermant, as it was codenamed, swung into action. In his biography, former Metropolitan Police commissioner, Sir John Stevens, wrote that the raid involved over 1,000 police officers. Most of the officers involved weren't informed of its true purpose but were encouraged to believe that it was an operation to arrest Abu Hamza.[6]

The mosque (which is in a residential street, near a busy main road) was surrounded by officers, who smashed open its doors and windows and poured inside. According to Stevens, their biggest fear was that the mosque had been booby-trapped with explosives, or that police would be rushed by a suicide bomber. However, instead of a suicide bomber poised to strike, police found eleven men asleep in the basement, who were understandably alarmed to be woken by the arrival of hundreds of police. All eleven were arrested and the mosque was systematically searched, which took the rest of the week.

Police recovered a stash of weapons and other suspect items from their search of the mosque: a CS gas spray canister, a stun gun, two blank-firing pistols, two knives, a chemical hazard suit, plus several false identification documents and numerous apparently bogus driving licences, credit cards and cheque books. It was certainly a highly dubious array of items to be kept at a building supposedly devoted to religious worship, but the finds were perhaps not as dramatic as police had been expecting. The only item which could be linked directly to the ricin plot was the mosque photocopier. Tests showed that the giant photocopy machine in the mosque offices had been used to make the copies of the poison recipes that had been recovered from Thetford.

On advice from his solicitor, Taleb answered most police questions with a 'no comment'. However, when the questioning turned to the matter of his fingerprint on the poison recipe, he was happy to provide an explanation: photocopying was one of his duties at the shop and he regularly copied items for customers without actually reading the material he had been given. Just because his fingerprint was on the back of one of the recipes didn't mean that he had ever actually seen it or knew what was in it, he insisted.

However, Taleb's portrayal of himself as an innocent bystander in any conspiracy was weakened after police found the CD-Rom computer disk containing bomb-making details. Although the police were never able to establish that he had definitely opened the file, its existence taken together with the fingerprint was enough for the prosecution to link Taleb to the conspiracy.

Mustapha Taleb was the last of the five ricin defendants to join the others in Belmarsh prison awaiting trial. By the time the case reached court 21 months later, Taleb was on antidepressants and his hair had fallen out from stress. His shaven-headedness was to make him look more menacing – particularly as it revealed a nasty scar on his head – but, ironically, his tough appearance was actually a reflection of what an ordeal he had found arrest and imprisonment, rather than of thuggishness.

6
Kamel Bourgass

On the morning of 8 January, news that ricin had been found in the Wood Green flat was splashed all over the UK media.

Most striking of all was the *Daily Mirror*, with its skull and crossbones and 'IT'S HERE' headline, which Bourgass's QC would brandish melodramatically during the trial.[1] In similar vein, the *Sun*, another tabloid newspaper, reported the discovery of a 'factory of death'[2]; while the *Daily Mail* reported that 'Security around the Prime Minister and members of the Royal Family ... remained tight.'[3]

Apart from creating unnecessary public fears, the lurid headlines also served to alert Kamel Bourgass to the fact that the police would be looking for him. Taking just a few possessions – little more than a copy of the Koran and his mobile phone – Bourgass left London and headed for Bournemouth, on the south coast. Along the way, he disposed of his SIM card, and replaced it with a new one, to stop police being able to trace him through his phone.

He arrived in Bournemouth on 8 January to look for an acquaintance who had a flat in the town. However, unable to find his contact, and having been turned away by the people who were living at the property, Bourgass ended up spending a night in a hotel.

The next day, he took a coach from the seaside town of Weymouth to Manchester, to look for another contact, Khaled Alwerfeli. Alwerfeli had a flat in Crumpsall Lane in the Cheetham Hill area of the city and, although Bourgass had met him only once before (having been introduced in London by Mohammed Meguerba), he was hopeful Alwerfeli would give him a bolthole.

At this stage, the police were indeed hunting for Bourgass, questioning the men they had arrested as a result of the Wood Green raid as to his likely whereabouts. On 12 January, they arrived at the address in Bournemouth that Bourgass had visited and arrested five men and one woman.

By now, Bourgass was already safely ensconced at Crumpsall Lane, and as police had no immediate way of linking him with Alwerfeli, it appeared Bourgass had made a clean getaway.

As he left London, there was nothing about Bourgass's unprepossessing appearance that would have aroused suspicion. He was slightly built, with short woolly hair. He looked to be in his late twenties or early thirties, although his exact age is unknown. Even now, little is known for certain about Bourgass's background, despite his having been extensively interrogated by police. During the course of police interviews, he has claimed various different names and nationalities and given different dates of birth. Many of his other claims are also difficult to verify. For example, he told UK police he had been a member of the Algerian police, but was not able to describe what a police identity card looks like.

Bourgass also claimed to have had brief spells of employment in the UK as a waiter in a pizza restaurant and a street cleaner. However, one fact that is known about him is that he was a prolific shoplifter and it is likely that the large amount of cash found at Feddag's flat were the proceeds of his thievery. Bourgass made a good living selling stolen clothes in and around the Finsbury Park Mosque and seems to have taken the business of stealing seriously. When police raided the Wood Green flat, they also found a stash of gold foil sweet wrappers that Bourgass used to wrap around electronic security tags to stop shop alarms being triggered, along with a pair of wire cutters for removing tags. His efforts to avoid detection were not always successful, however. In July 2002, Bourgass had been arrested and bailed for stealing a pair of jeans from a shop in Romford.

As well as bringing him to the notice of the police, Bourgass's shoplifting also led to his first contact with Mohammed Meguerba when, in spring 2002, he sold Meguerba some clothing at the mosque. The pair rapidly struck up what was to become a fateful friendship.

Bourgass – who had come to the UK in January 2000 – also met Sidali Feddag some time in 2002. Although they weren't close associates, Feddag would nod hello to Bourgass when he saw him selling things around the mosque. Feddag would have been aware of Bourgass's thieving but it didn't deter him from offering Bourgass use of his room after the clampdown on men sleeping at the mosque in summer 2002. In the morally fuzzy world of the illegal immigrant, Feddag saw Bourgass's stealing as necessary for survival, rather than anything to be deprecated.

Bourgass stayed at Feddag's flat until December when he was asked to leave to make room for one of Feddag's brothers who was arriving from Algeria. Bourgass complied but left behind the panoply of incriminating items, as well as over £4,000 in cash.

Where Bourgass went after he left Feddag's flat has never been fully established. He claimed to have stayed at two different hotels, although maintained in court he couldn't remember their names or locations, nor what name he registered under. It seems more likely that Bourgass simply flouted the ban imposed by the trustees and went back to sleeping at the mosque, before landing up in Manchester on 9 January.

After failing to find him in Bournemouth, police had no further leads and it was pure chance that they stumbled across Bourgass at the Crumpsall Lane flat five days later. In the wake of the raid in Wood Green, Home Secretary David Blunkett had ordered the arrest and detention of another terrorist suspect who, for legal reasons, can only be identified as Q.

Q, who was not associated with the ricin plot, was linked to two addresses, one of which was Alwerfeli's Crumpsall Lane flat, and a big police operation was launched to arrest him. The 24 officers involved – drawn from the Tactical Aid Unit (TAU), Manchester Police and Special Branch – were given a briefing about the impending raid by Special Branch officer 'Simon' in the car park at Collyhurst police station. One TAU officer later described the briefing as the worst he had ever attended. The car park was noisy, with police vehicles constantly moving around, and because it was impossible to hear what was being said, the officer had to ask a colleague to fill in the details later.

At Bourgass's subsequent trial for murdering DC Stephen Oake during the raid, prosecuting barrister Nigel Sweeney QC was equally damning. He told the court, there was 'no final or sufficient risk assessment, no written operational order as would be expected, a lack of clear briefing about individuals' roles in the raid and not enough information about the targets or contingency planning if someone else turned out to be in the flat'.

Channel frequencies on the police radios were not identified, as was customary, and officers had to use their mobile phones to communicate with each other. They were given no clear direction as to which of the flats in the three-storey Victorian house was Alwerfeli's.

If the briefing was shambolic, the execution of the raid was to be even worse. The three teams of TAU officers, wearing body armour and specially trained in entry and search methods, were ordered to stay outside the building to deal with any possible public unrest. The Special Branch officers, wearing civilian clothes, entered the flat and were surprised to find, not just Q and Alwerfeli in the flat, but another man as well. When asked for his name, he wrote down in English: 'Kamel Bourgass, 5 May 1975, Asylum.'

Bourgass, of course, had many aliases and his choice of this particular name was crucial to what happened next. He had been living in London as Nadir Habra (the name he reverted to during the ricin trial, although he was charged as Kamel Bourgass) and Sidali Feddag had told police that the suspect items belonged to his flatmate 'Nadir'. Police would also have had a record of Nadir Habra's having been arrested for shoplifting in Romford and of him as a failed asylum seeker. By contrast, the name Kamel Bourgass was unknown to police and raised no immediate suspicions. Officers did, however, note a resemblance between Bourgass and the description of the man wanted following the Wood Green raid. They contacted the anti-terror police in London and were sent a photograph of the suspect, showing he had a distinctive mole on his top lip, which matched the one they could see on the man they were holding. Only then did officers realise they had unwittingly captured another major terrorist suspect, wanted in connection with discovery of the Wood Green 'factory of death'.

Alwerfeli was held in the sitting room, while Bourgass and Q were kept in the bedroom. None of the men was handcuffed. A decision had been made not to bring special terror-suspect arrest kits into Crumpsall Lane, which would have included bags for the men's hands and feet (to preserve evidence), and plastic restraint ties. It is still not clear why the men weren't restrained. One newspaper suggested the men were left untied because police feared a display of force might stir up the local Muslim community – but there is no evidence to support this claim.

Whatever the reason, the decision to leave the suspects unrestrained was to have dreadful consequences. Bourgass had been told to stay in the bedroom with Q, where both men were guarded by Detective Constable Stephen Oake. Oake was casually dressed in a rugby shirt, and not wearing any kind of body armour or anti-stab vest. Oake had not been told that Bourgass was being linked to the Wood Green raid. Special Branch had a 'need to know' policy and the man guarding the suspect did not, apparently, need to know. Thirty minutes after police arrived at the flat, Bourgass was arrested under the Terrorism Act on suspicion of being involved with the ricin plot. Another officer, Nigel Flemming, who had been with the TAU for just eleven weeks, volunteered to watch Bourgass and Q while they waited for the arrival of sterile transportation which would preserve any incriminating evidence on the three suspects.

By now, it was 4.55 p.m., an hour since the initial raid. Bourgass was beginning to get agitated, talking to Q in

Arabic. Flemming told him to stop talking and tried to calm him down – but the officer's intervention seemed to have the opposite effect. Bourgass lashed out, punching Flemming in the groin and then charged out of the bedroom. He rushed into the kitchen, but there was no escape from there as the window was too small. Bourgass was now frantic to get away. He grabbed a kitchen knife with a five-inch blade from the draining board, and began wielding it at the officers, while trying to get make his way to the front door. The raid had clearly gone badly wrong. It was a tiny flat and the large number of officers crammed into it made it more chaotic. Somehow, the lights went out, creating even more confusion.

DC Oake grabbed Bourgass from behind, holding him in a bear hug, to try to stop him getting away. Bourgass repeatedly stabbed at Oake with the knife, but still the officer held him. Three other officers were also knifed by Bourgass in what was later described as a rugby scrum. Despite his slight frame and the number of officers trying to restrain him, Bourgass made it as far as the landing outside the flat door before finally being overpowered and handcuffed.

By the time Bourgass was finally subdued, the scene at the flat was one of carnage – with blood spattered over the sitting-room walls and on the outside landing. Oake – who held on to Bourgass throughout – had been stabbed eight times in the chest, including through the heart and lungs, and was bleeding profusely. Three of the wounds were so violently inflicted that any single one of them could have been fatal. He was given emergency medical treatment by fellow officers and an ambulance was called but he died at the scene. DC Oake left a widow and three young children.

The Crumpsall Lane raid had been a disaster and attracted widespread condemnation. Several of the officers involved later criticised the lack of coordination. Sergeant Grindrod, one of the TAU team wounded by Bourgass, said with remarkable understatement: 'Certain officers believe there was a shortfall in the planning of the operation.'

A TAU officer who had been guarding Alwerfeli in the sitting room of the flat stated in court: 'I expected the man to be handcuffed. I offered to handcuff him on the other officer's behalf. The offer was declined. I was surprised. The man was just in the room with myself and PC 'B'. I was not happy. He had been arrested and we were just stood there and obviously there was a safety concern.'

The raid was investigated by the West Midlands Police, Merseyside Police and the Health and Safety Executive and was roundly condemned by all of them. At Bourgass's subsequent trial for the murder of DC Oake, his barrister Michel Massih QC sought to blame the police's lack of organisation for his client's violent behaviour. 'It's a death that should never have occurred and would never have occurred but for the actions of certain individual officers in that tiny little flat. It was triggered in conditions we say were total police chaos, mismanagement at the highest levels. Chaos reigned.'

The press was banned from reporting any aspect of the murder case to avoid prejudicing the subsequent ricin trial (which is why none of the jurors in the latter case knew that one of the defendants was a convicted murderer). However, the murder trial jurors were told of Bourgass's involvement in the ricin plot as proof of his state of mind and why he was so desperate to escape.

Although Bourgass did take the witness stand at the ricin trial (he was one of only two of the five defendants to do so), he did not give evidence at the murder trial. His barrister told the court that he had lashed out because the officer guarding him, Flemming, had been racist and aggressive towards him (claims rejected by other witnesses). He said Bourgass had been panicked by the police raid, and reacted out of fear for his own life. Once trapped in the kitchen, he had acted in self-defence, injuring officers unintentionally in the ensuing chaos; he had not meant to hurt anyone and deeply regretted his actions.

In June 2004, after an eleven-week trial at the Old Bailey, Bourgass was convicted of all charges. He was sentenced to life imprisonment for DC Oake's murder, with a recommendation he serve a minimum of 20 years and six months. He received concurrent sentences of 15 years each for the attempted murder of the other officers and seven years for wounding with intent.

DC Stephen Oake was later nominated for a posthumous George Cross, the highest civilian award for valour. His nomination was refused on the grounds that Oake's actions were not sufficiently heroic to warrant the award. The reaction from his local police force was one of understandable outrage. Paul Kelly, chairman of Greater Manchester Police Federation, described it as 'an absolute insult to the memory of Stephen, his family and every police officer in Britain'. He added that Oake had been brutally murdered by an 'utterly evil, dangerous man', who had already stabbed and very nearly killed a colleague. 'Stephen chose to intervene, even though he was unarmed and wearing no protective equipment.'[4] The other three wounded officers all later sued for compensation for their injuries.

Kelly's description of Bourgass as evil and dangerous is certainly warranted. With the murder of Stephen Oake and the injuries he inflicted on the other officers, Bourgass showed himself fully capable of murderous brutality. However, whether he was also the single-minded master terrorist portrayed by the prosecution in the ricin case is less clear.

Bourgass's activities were in the main notable for their amateurishness, bungling and pointless risk-taking, rather than ruthless calculation. He was an organised and dedicated shoplifter (although he sometimes stole things which he could neither use nor resell, such as dishwasher powder) – but took a rather more casual approach to his terrorist plotting. He continued to be a prolific shoplifter, even though it put him at constant risk of arrest and discovery of his other activities. Even after his run-in with police in Romford, where he narrowly avoided deportation as an illegal immigrant, he continued to steal.

For someone plotting a terrorist attack, Bourgass left much to chance and had few, if any, contingency plans. He meekly complied with Sidali Feddag's request that he vacate the flat, even though he had nowhere else to go and it meant leaving behind the tools of his terrorist trade, where they could easily be discovered. He also left behind over £4,000 in cash locked in a bag – but with the key in the outside pocket.

When Bourgass fled London, again, he had no clear plan of where to go next. He headed for Bournemouth but, rather than finding the sanctuary he was hoping for, was unceremoniously turned away by the occupants of the house. (If he had been allowed to stay, he would almost certainly have been picked up just four days later, when police raided the house looking for him.)

Bourgass chose to take the witness stand at the ricin trial but did not make an ideal witness. Whereas the other defendants generally wore a shirt and tie, Bourgass was always scruffily dressed. He wrong-footed his own barrister by announcing that he wasn't Kamel Bourgass (the name he had been charged under) but Nadir Habra. His demeanour during questioning was a mix of arrogance and indifference, changing his story as he went along. At times, he became angry with the prosecution barrister.

Bourgass claimed in court that all the suspect items (including the recipes) belonged to the absent Meguerba. However, in his oral statement to police in 2003, he had given a different explanation. At that point, he claimed to have found the items in a bag lying in a street in Brixton, south London. He said he had later disposed of the bag but hung on to its contents even though he knew they were dangerous. When police asked why he hadn't got rid of them as well, he replied: 'Because I am stupid.'

Despite the endless lies that he told, for once it seems Bourgass may have been telling the truth.

7
What Ricin?

On the 5 February 2003, Colin Powell, then US Secretary of State, addressed the United Nations Security Council to argue the case for war against Iraq. Among the reasons he cited was Iraq's refusal to handover its weapons of mass destruction and what he described as 'a sinister nexus' between Iraq and Al-Qaeda. Powell claimed that Abu Musab Al-Zarqawi, a Palestinian who had fought in Afghanistan in the 1990s, was running a terrorist training camp in north eastern Iraq. Al-Zarqawi was a suspected collaborator with Osama bin Laden and supposedly an expert in poisons, including ricin.

In an emotive speech, Powell told the Security Council: 'Let me remind you how ricin works. Less than a pinch – imagine a pinch of salt – less than a pinch of ricin, eating just this amount in your food would cause shock followed by circulatory failure. Death comes within 72 hours and there is no antidote. There is no cure. It is fatal.'[1]

As a slide headed 'Al-Zarqawi's Iraq-Linked Terrorist Network' was projected on to a screen above him, Powell went on: 'The chart you are seeing shows the network in Europe. We know about this European network, and we know about its links to Zarqawi, because the detainee who provided the information about the targets also provided the names of members of the network. Three of those he identified by name were arrested in France last December. In the apartments of the terrorists, authorities found circuits for explosive devices and a list of ingredients to make toxins. The detainee who helped piece this together says the plot also targeted Britain. Later evidence, again, proved him right. When the British unearthed a cell there just last month, one British police officer was murdered during the disruption of the cell.'

The detainee in question was likely to have been Mohammed Meguerba, being held by the Algerian authorities; the murdered police officer was DC Stephen Oake, stabbed to death by Kamel Bourgass. Within weeks of the Wood Green raid, the 'ricin plot' was being used by the highest levels of the American administration to bolster the case for war against Iraq.

Powell got his facts about ricin wrong – it is relatively ineffective if administered via food – but his argument was persuasive enough for the Security Council to ratify resolution 1441, allowing military force against Iraq for failing to give up its weapons of mass destruction. Given the formal blessing of the UN, the US and Britain went to war with Iraq within a matter of weeks.

What Powell may genuinely not have known was that, despite claims to the contrary, British police had not actually found any ricin at all.

Powell's confusion was understandable. A month before his address to the Security Council, Metropolitan Police Assistant Commissioner David Veness and Deputy Chief Medical Officer Dr Pat Troop issued a joint statement confirming the discovery of a noxious substance during the police raid on Sidali Feddag's flat. 'A small amount of the material recovered from the Wood Green premises has tested positive for the presence of ricin poison. Tests were carried out on the material and it was confirmed this morning that toxic material was present. The Department [of Health] is now alerting the health service, including primary care, about these developments.'[2]

Prime Minister Tony Blair weighed in later the same day, telling a meeting of British ambassadors in London: 'The arrests which were made show this danger is present and real and with us now. Its potential is huge.'[3] Home Secretary David Blunkett and Health Secretary John Reid also issued a joint statement claiming 'traces of ricin' and enough castor oil beans to make 'one lethal dose' had been discovered.

Despite such comments by individuals supposedly in a position to know, just two days after the Wood Green raid there was evidence that earlier indications ricin had been found might have been wrong. After a further battery of tests by government scientists, it was definitively established three weeks after the raid there were no traces of toxins on any of the equipment at the flat. Yet Porton Down did not pass on this information to government ministers and the police until 20 March. No full explanation has ever been given for this failure. The BBC was later to report that a Ministry of Defence spokesman blamed the delay on 'a breakdown in communications'.

The public had to wait even longer to learn the true facts. The myth of the Wood Green 'ricin find' was left publicly uncorrected until 2005 – although this was partly as a result of a legal embargo on reporting the case following Kamel Bourgass's arrest in Manchester on 14 January 2003.

Once the ricin story had been set running, it proved remarkably difficult to stop, even among those who should have known the truth. In October 2002, when UK anti-terror detectives were finally given permission to interview Mohammed Meguerba in Algeria, they were still referring to a definite ricin find at Wood Green.

A more recent example of the pervasiveness of the myth is in the 2009 autobiography of the former commissioner of the Metropolitan Police, Sir Ian Blair, where he cites the ricin plot as one of the 'major cases' which show the need for police to be able to hold suspects for longer without charge. 'If, in any of these cases, we had had to make early arrests, the then current fourteen-day limit would have been insufficient', he says.

Blair adds that police were hamstrung by fighting 'twenty-first terrorism with nineteenth-century legislation'. He cites the example of Kamel Bourgass who 'had to be charged with the nineteenth-century statute of public nuisance in attempting to administer a noxious substance'. Blair makes no mention of the fact that four of those tried alongside Bourgass were acquitted or that no ricin was ever actually found in the case.[4]

When the reporting ban was lifted after the ricin trial, Liberal Democrat defence spokesman Michael Moore said it was 'staggering' that the authorities were not told immediately it was clear there was no ricin, 'not least when it became so central to the political justification for war in Iraq'.[5]

Whether it arose by accident or design, such a potent misconception was undeniably useful to politicians trying to drum up support for an unpopular war, and for curtailing civil liberties in the fight against terrorism. Arguably, the early claims that ricin had been found had a distorting effect on the response of the authorities, media and public to the case from the start. In such a heightened atmosphere, it was far more difficult to take a measured and objective view about what the finds at the flat actually signified.

The very name 'ricin' is enough to create fear among the population. It is a poison whose deadly reputation goes before it in the popular imagination. In recent years it has been employed by authors and dramatists to great effect, featuring, for example, in Val McDermid's book *Beneath the Bleeding*[6] and in an episode of ITV's prison series *Bad Girls*.[7]

Many people in the UK will have first heard of the toxin after the 1978 murder of Bulgarian dissident writer Georgi Markov, who was killed by the KGB using an umbrella tip poisoned with ricin. Markov, who had survived previous assassination attempts, was waiting for a bus near London's Waterloo Bridge on his way to the BBC World Service where he worked, when he was jabbed in the calf by a man with an umbrella. The man apologised in a foreign accent before walking away. That evening Markov developed a high fever and was admitted to hospital. Two days later, he was dead. On post-mortem, it was discovered that the cause of death was ricin poisoning, administered via the umbrella tip, which had been used to inject a ricin-filled pellet the size of a pinhead into Markov's leg. Even if his doctors had realised sooner what was making him ill, they still could have done nothing as there is no known antidote.

Ricin is an extremely deadly substance – twice as lethal as cobra venom – but it is an unlikely choice for terrorists, particularly terrorists as amateurish as Bourgass. It is more suitable for a meticulously planned and carefully targeted assassination (as in the Markov case), rather than for killing indiscriminately on a wide scale.

As Dr A, the Porton Down expert, told the Old Bailey trial, to cause certain death, ricin needs to be either injected directly into the bloodstream or inhaled. Dr Alastair Hay, Professor of Environmental Toxicology at the University of Leeds, said in an article in the *Independent on Sunday*, published after the end of the ricin trial in April 2005, that simply swallowing ricin is 'a thousand times less effective than by injection'.[8]

Even if Bourgass was serious about manufacturing ricin, it seems he didn't know much about how it works, as his recipes talked about adding it to food or mixing it with cosmetic oil to poison through the skin.

Bourgass was not alone in his ignorance about ricin's properties. It was shared not just by Colin Powell and some newspapers (the *Daily Mail* reported the plan was to smear it on door handles) but also the prosecution at the trial. Prosecution barrister Nigel Sweeney pointed to three new toothbrushes found in a bag belonging to Bourgass, where the packaging had been tampered with (but was still intact). Sweeney suggested Bourgass planned to smear ricin on the brush heads and then put them back in shops for people to buy. Whereas the *Sun* described the assassination of Markov with a poisoned umbrella as 'straight out of James Bond',[9] Bourgass's activities smacked more of Inspector Clouseau.

Whatever his plan, it's unlikely that Bourgass would have succeeded in manufacturing ricin by using the recipes and equipment that he had accumulated at Wood Green, as ricin is extremely difficult to manufacture outside a laboratory. There are simpler and more readily available ways of killing people, if that is your intent. To paraphrase Bourgass's defence barrister, Michel Massih QC: Feddag's flat was directly above a pharmacy; if Bourgass wanted to kill anyone, why go to all the trouble of making ricin when he could simply nip downstairs and buy rat poison.

8
Backlash

'*Read the Daily Mail tomorrow; you'll be amazed at what you missed...*'. When the jurors did read the newspapers the day after the ricin trial, they understood what the usher had meant by her remark as they had filed out of the courtroom for the last time.

To avoid prejudicing the case, the media had been banned from reporting Kamel Bourgass's earlier conviction for the killing of DC Stephen Oake. With the ricin trial concluded the day before, on 14 April the press was finally free to publish the full story. The murder of a police officer is always a big story in Britain, as such killings are mercifully rare. The fact that DC Oake had been brutally killed during the bungled arrest of a terror suspect only added to the media's interest.

The *Daily Mail* led with a picture of DC Oake, alongside the headline: 'Murdered because we've lost control of our borders'. The *Mail*'s story blamed DC Oake's death on the UK's overloaded and failing immigration system. Bourgass had 'no right to be in the country', and 'Britain's porous borders' were to blame. A *Mail* editorial slammed Labour's immigration policy: 'This trained Algerian agent for Al-Qaeda had one aim when he waltzed unchecked into Britain: to kill people on an industrial scale. An expert in poisons, he was up to his neck in a plot to manufacture ricin and other deadly substances. And what was to stop him? Certainly not the Government's pitifully inept policies.'[1]

The revelation that Bourgass was a convicted police killer caused shock and consternation among the jurors. Some were distraught to think they had spent six months sitting so close to a brutal murderer (at one point, all twelve of the security guards in the dock with him appeared to be asleep); and one juror was almost in tears, thinking about DC Oake's now fatherless young children.

Other papers took a similar line to the *Mail*. The *Daily Express* reported that DC Oake had been murdered 'because police would not handcuff a Muslim'[2] (although there was no evidence to support this explanation). The *Daily Mirror* labelled Bourgass 'The Toxic Terrorist'. Over a three-page article, the paper spelled out how 'the gang of men ...[was] preparing for jihad in Britain'. Their plan was to 'produce a poison which can kill 80,000 people with just ONE GRAM'.[3]

The *Mirror* article included a photograph of batteries, torch bulbs and odd bits of wire from the Wood Green flat. It was labelled: 'Electrical components. Enough kit to make several explosive devices.' No such thing had ever been suggested in court. Rather than material for making bombs, the items were most likely the results of Bourgass's indiscriminate shoplifting. A more accurate caption might have read: 'Electrical components. Enough kit to mend several torches.' A picture showing black onion seeds found in a wardrobe was labelled: 'May have been for a deadly recipe.' Again, this had never been suggested in the trial, where it was accepted the onion seeds were genuinely for use in herbal remedies.

In a *Daily Mirror* photo, Bourgass looked very different from the mild-mannered and bespectacled figure he cut at the trial. This one showed him unshaven, hollow-cheeked and with cropped hair. His face showed heavy bruising, presumably a legacy of his violent escape attempt and the deadly attack on DC Oake.

The biggest shock for the former jurors was that Bourgass was described as an Al-Qaeda operative, a claim which had never been made in court. According to the *Sun*, Bourgass had been 'unmasked as Osama bin Laden's master poisoner – with a mission to murder as many Britons as possible'.[4] Unmasked how and by whom was not specified.

The *Sun* was not alone in making wild assertions. Most of the media reported Mohammed Meguerba and Bourgass's 'Al-Qaeda connection' as fact. What wasn't reported was that the only basis for such a claim was Meguerba's highly dubious 'confession' to the Algerian police. Even though the prosecution at the trial had accepted Meguerba was a liar and his evidence unreliable, none of the newspapers questioned the idea that the pair were Al-Qaeda operatives.

The one-sided media coverage was not surprising. Despite its political significance, there had been minimal press presence during the trial. On some days, the press box was completely empty, with the media relying on Crown Prosecution Service press releases and information from the police. Significantly, there were no journalists in court to hear Michael Mansfield QC's demolition of Porton Down operations manager Andrew Gould's testimony. As a result, the revelation that no ricin had ever been found at the so-called 'factory of death' (and that this was known two days after the raid) went unreported and largely unnoticed.

It has never been satisfactorily explained why Porton Down did not pass on the key information about the lack of any ricin. After Gould's revelation in court that he had wrongly told police ricin had been detected, the judge sent him away to check his computer records to try to establish how the confusion had arisen. Both he and the witness known as 'Dr A' – the Porton Down scientist who had established there was no ricin – had then been recalled to give evidence for a second time. Dr A was as calm and collected during his reappearance in the witness box as he had been the first time around. As requested, he had checked back through his computer records and had found two emails which he had sent to Gould confirming that the tests for ricin had come back negative.

Gould, on the other hand, insisted in his evidence that he had no recollection of ever receiving Dr A's emails: he must have deleted both messages without ever having read them, he suggested.

Whether it was solely down to Gould that the police and media were wrongly told that ricin had been found when it hadn't, or whether there was a more sinister explanation, has never been established. However it came about, through cock-up or conspiracy, the 'ricin myth' was certainly useful to those making the case for war and arguing for further restrictions on civil liberties.

As Mark Twain said, a lie can travel halfway around the world before the truth has got its shoes on, and the ricin myth took on such a life of its own that it refused to die, even after the facts were (or should have been) widely known. As recently as February 2006, the then Chancellor Gordon Brown referred to the 'ricin chemical plot', in a speech to the Royal United Services Institute about fighting global terrorism, claiming the investigation of the plot had spanned 26 countries.

In the aftermath of the trial, the tenor of the media coverage was that the acquitted men had 'got away with it', and that the case showed that Britain was under threat from Al-Qaeda – despite no evidence having been put forward for this.

It was a view of the trial apparently shared by politicians and senior police officers. A few days after its conclusion, the then Commissioner for the Metropolitan Police, Sir Ian Blair, told the BBC TVs *Breakfast with Frost*: 'There's real clarity now that Al-Qaeda affiliates are targeting Britain.' Following the acquittals, it was time to look again at 'how the legal system deals with cases of this sort'. Blair suggested the men might have been acquitted because of flaws in legal procedures. 'It's been a very long time coming to trial; it was a hugely long trial, and I think there will be a number of questions to be asked, whether the law is quite right. ... The way that Al-Qaeda operates, is in a sense of very loose knit conspiracies, and in comparison to the United States, for instance, or Continental law, the way English law has developed, it doesn't like conspiracies, it likes, actual, offences ... and where one person does something, another person does another thing, it's only when they add up that they become a conspiracy. I think that's when you look for the kind of acquittal that we've seen. I think we're just going to have to just look again, to see whether there's some other legislation, around "acts preparatory to terrorism" or something of that nature, that's what we'll have to do.'[5]

Home Secretary Charles Clarke told the media the case showed 'there are terrorist organisations which seek to challenge us in this country and challenge our basic freedom'. He denied that the acquittal of four of the five Algerians and the abandonment of the subsequent trial of four others also accused of being part of the plot was an embarrassment. 'We will obviously keep a very close eye on the eight men being freed today, and consider exactly what to do in the light of this decision', he said.[6]

Peter Clarke, head of the anti-terror police told the press: 'This was a hugely serious plot because what it had the potential to do was to cause real panic, fear, disruption and possibly even death.'[7]

The 'Al-Qaeda conspiracy' that the media were reporting bore little relationship to the case heard in court. Unlike the politicians and journalists, the jurors had listened to every bit of evidence over the six months of the trial and spent 17 days deliberating before arriving at their verdicts. Now, they must have felt as if they were the ones in the dock: facing accusations of naivety or having been duped (there were even mutterings in some quarters that the jury had 'gone rogue').

One of the few journalists to take a detailed interest in the case all the way through was the investigative writer Duncan Campbell, who also acts as a scientific expert witness on computers and telecommunications. Campbell had acted as an advisor to the defence, debunking the prosecution claim that Bourgass's recipes emanated from an Al-Qaeda training manual by showing that the recipes were drawn from the internet and other readily available sources.

At the end of the trial, Campbell wrote a withering article about the ensuing misreporting. Under the headline: 'The ricin ring that never was', he described Bourgass as 'an Islamist yobbo' acting on his own, rather than 'an Al-Qaeda trained superterrorist'. 'An ASBO might be appropriate', he added.[8]

Although the coverage that greeted the end of the trial came as a shock to the jurors, over-heated and over-egged reporting of the case dated back to the first arrests in 2002 and had continued on and off throughout. On 17 November, the day before Mouloud Sihali and David Khalef were charged with possessing false identity documents, they were described as suspected Al-Qaeda terrorists who, it was variously reported, planned to gas an underground train, release cyanide, or to plant a dirty bomb on a ferry.

Soon after the Wood Green raid, the BBC News website carried an article asking: 'Is the NHS ready for ricin victims?'[9] Its clear conclusion was that the health service was dangerously unprepared for large numbers of poison victims. 'Public health experts say the system for alerting hospitals and GPs about health risks has worked. But an intensive care consultant, one of those who should have been informed, told the BBC the only information he had received had come via the media. He said "... if there was to be a major health risk ... it could be several days, maybe a week or two before key practitioners actually found the details."' Dr Sue Atkinson, director of public health for London, was quoted saying people should not panic. 'The important thing is ... to be alert to these things. But we don't want people to be alarmed.'

When the BBC ran the article, it had no way of knowing that Porton Down had already established that no ricin had been found. Earlier comments by then Home Secretary David Blunkett were, however, less understandable or forgivable. On 14 November 2004, when the case was in full swing at the Old Bailey (and with the trial of the second batch of defendants expected to follow on immediately afterwards), Blunkett told the media: 'Al-Qaeda ... will be demonstrated through the courts in months to come, to be actually on our doorstep and threatening our lives. I am talking about people who are and [are] about to go through the court system.'[10]

Linking the defendants with Al-Qaeda (when no such claim was ever made to the jury at the ongoing trial) was an extraordinarily prejudicial intervention for the Home Secretary to make. The trial judge complained about Blunkett's remarks to the attorney general, Peter Goldsmith QC, who rebuked the Home Secretary and warned him not to make a repetition.

It was not the first time that Blunkett had intervened in the ricin case. In 2002, after the arrests of David Khalef and Mouloud Sihali, while dismissing some of the more outlandish media coverage, Blunkett told BBC Radio 4's *Today* programme that the police had 'picked up those who, quite separately from any nonsense about gas attacks, actually were planning to set up a cell to threaten our country'.[11]

The leading human rights lawyer, Gareth Peirce, who was acting for Khalef and Sihali, responded by accusing Blunkett of contempt of court. She was, she said, stunned 'by this quite extraordinary tidal wave of completely contemptuous and prejudicial coverage'.[12]

Peirce also punctured claims of a major terrorist conspiracy by neatly summing up what the 'ricin plot' had actually consisted of: 'There never was any ricin; there were no poisons made. There seems to have been a pathetic, clumsy, amateurish attempt to make some by a man who was conceded, I think by all, to be a difficult anti-social loner.'

She questioned how it was that 'all of us in this country' were allowed to believe there had been a 'substantial plot', rather than the 'individualist, tiny, failed attempt', that it was.[13]

At every stage, the 'ricin plot' had been hijacked for political purposes. From the initial arrests of Khalef and Sihali, to discovery of the so-called 'factory of death', and subsequent trial and acquittals, the case was cited by those arguing for restrictions on civil liberties and by politicians seeking to bolster the case for war against Iraq.

In another example of government over-egging the extent of the plot, the Home Office was forced to write letters of apology to ten former Belmarsh detainees, whom it had wrongly claimed were linked to the ricin plot. When the ten were released and put on control orders, the original grounds cited were that they 'belonged to and have provided support for a network of North African extremists directly involved in terrorist planning in the UK, including the use of toxic chemicals'. The Home Office was forced to revise the orders and blamed a 'clerical error' for getting the grounds on the original orders wrong. A solicitor for one of the former detainees commented: 'I couldn't believe an organisation such as the Home Office could make that mistake. It's obviously someone sitting there doing a cut and paste job.'[14]

Michael Mansfield QC, who had acted for Mouloud Sihali, was also concerned about the case being hijacked for political ends. He recounts in his memoirs that he feared the 'unacceptable' verdict in the trial would be used as an excuse for a broader assault on the jury system. 'So much so that I and many others at the Bar were concerned that the government would use this as an excuse to promote non-jury trials for terrorist-related cases.'[15]

Once the verdict was announced, the case was seized upon by those arguing in favour of the government's controversial (and ultimately unsuccessful) proposal for terror suspects to be held for 90 days without charge.

An October 2005 briefing note written for the Select Committee on Home Affairs by Peter Clarke, head of the anti-terror police, sought to blame the acquittals on the police not having enough time to investigate before either charging or releasing suspects. 'Had there been the opportunity to understand the complexities of the conspiracy before the decision was required to charge or release, the right charges against the right people could have been determined from the outset. The quality of the original charging decisions would also have been higher, and it is probable that the suspect who fled the country while on bail and who eventually proved to have been a prime conspirator, would have stood trial in this country. If that had happened, the outcome of the trial process might have been very different.'[16]

The 'suspect who fled the country' was an obvious reference to Mohammed Meguerba. But as the Liberal Democrat MP Lynne Featherstone – a prominent critic of government's counter-terror policies – was to point out, Meguerba's was an odd case to cite in support of holding suspects for longer. Writing in her blog of 12 November 2006, Featherstone pointed out that Meguerba was actually released after only *two* days, so even under the current laws, 'the police could have kept him in detention for much longer if they'd wanted to'. If, as Clarke suggested, Meguerba really was the kind of major terrorist whose existence necessitated a change in the law to allow detention without charge for 90 days, 'why did the police let him go after just two?'

A sizeable group of the former jurors had kept in touch in the immediate aftermath of the trial. The case had been an intense and demanding experience; reading the subsequent press coverage about DC Oake's murder and the supposed Al-Qaeda connection was upsetting and unsettling. They met up a few times to share thoughts about the trial and what they'd read in the press, but before long, having already devoted six months of their lives to the case, most jurors wanted life to return to normal and for the case to fade into the background.

However, a few of them, including the 51-year-old telephone engineer who had acted as foreman, couldn't let the case drop. This small diehard group kept in touch and kept on worrying away at the implications of the trial, sharing whatever information they could find out.

They began to research the background to the case and the defendants on the internet – something they had been forbidden from doing during the trial. They uncovered a wealth of information: some of it plainly fantastical nonsense; some of it more plausible. The more they read, however, the more they wanted to know. What evidence was there that Bourgass was an Al-Qaeda operative? What had they missed during the many times when the trial had been adjourned for legal arguments? They understood that potentially prejudicial material had to be kept from them while the trial was going on, but why couldn't they be told now? It felt as though everyone else had more information about 'their' case than they did.

The jurors tried contacting the Old Bailey, and then the lawyers who had acted for the defendants for information. Each time, they were soundly rebuffed. There were no official channels that would recognise their interest in the case, or provide any information.

They rapidly learned that, although jurors are required to hang on every word of a case for the life of the trial (and there are stringent penalties for those who don't take their role seriously), their interest is not expected to outlive delivery of the verdict. No matter what demands a trial may have made on jurors, often over months, the justice system loses interest in them the minute the trial has ended.

Eventually, their sheer bloody-mindedness and refusal to give up led them into contact with two sympathetic journalists who had followed the case. It's quite a novelty for reporters to be sought out by jurors and the pair were generous with their time and their information, spending many hours talking to the jurors – who were left reeling by what they learned.

The jurors were told that Meguerba – who had been mentioned throughout the trial – was being held by the Algerian authorities. For the first time, they learned about Algeria's appalling record on human rights and that there was plausible evidence that Meguerba had been brutally tortured into making his confession. The police investigation which sparked the arrests and much of the subsequent prosecution case had been built on evidence obtained from the Algerians by coercion. They also learned that Meguerba had fled to Algeria after being arrested and then rapidly released by British anti-terror police.

The case had been marked by long periods when the jurors were sent out of the court and then recalled, with no explanation given for the delay. Now they learned that much of this time had been taken up with legal arguments over whether the judge should allow Meguerba's evidence to be put directly to the jury.

Lawyers acting for two of the defendants, Feddag and Sihali, had tried to persuade the judge that Meguerba's testimony should be included. Meguerba had given his Algerian interrogators a string of names of supposed fellow conspirators, which seemed to include just about every fellow Algerian he had come across during his time in London (including Bourgass, Taleb and Khalef) – but there was no mention of Feddag or Sihali. The pair's lawyers argued this omission strengthened their clients' claim not to have been part of any terrorist conspiracy, if such a thing existed.

Interestingly, it was prosecution barrister Nigel Sweeney QC who argued against its inclusion on the basis that Meguerba was a liar and his evidence unreliable. The judge, Mr Justice Penry-Davey, eventually declared the Meguerba evidence inadmissible and it was never put before the jury. Repeated requests by the defence to be allowed to interview Meguerba in Algeria were equally unsuccessful.

What the jurors learned about Sweeney's damning assessment in court of Meguerba's reliability struck them as curious, given they now knew how much weight had been placed on Meguerba's evidence both before and after the trial: it had led police to the 'factory of death'; and was the source for widely reported claims about the Al-Qaeda connection.

Having finally found someone who took their interest in the case seriously and who would talk to them, that might have been the end of the jurors' involvement in the case, were it not for what happened next.

After the trial and his conviction for conspiracy to cause a public nuisance, Kamel Bourgass was returned to prison where he was already serving a life sentence for the murder of DC Oake. Mustapha Taleb, the only defendant with the legal right to be in the UK, was released immediately. The other three, who had all entered the country illegally, were remanded into immigration detention. After a few days, they were bailed, having already served enough time in custody to account for the sentences they had received for holding false ID documents.

If the defendants were hoping the worst was over, they were to be disappointed. At the end of the trial, Home Secretary

Charles Clarke had warned he would keeping 'a very close eye' on the freed men – and he was as good as his word.

On 14 May, the *Guardian* ran a story under the heading: 'Cleared ricin suspects face deportation'. The jurors read the story with an increasing sense of disbelief and anger. Having earlier faced accusations of naivety or worse, this seemed to be a far more serious example of the jury's long-considered verdict being disregarded.

The *Guardian* reported that the government was seeking to deport the acquitted men, despite the very real danger they would be tortured on their return to Algeria. 'The men have all been granted bail but, according to their lawyers, the Home Office is "not giving an inch" in its attempt to send them to what could be their deaths.'[17]

From what the jurors now knew about Algeria's human rights record, they had good reason to believe that men branded Islamic terrorists by Britain would be in danger if they were returned. Having held the men's fate in their hands during the trial, they still felt a degree of responsibility for them now.

For the jurors, this was an apocalyptic moment: a turning point in their lives. They had been obliged to do jury service as part of their civic duty; they had duly put their working lives on hold for six months while they sat on a difficult and demanding case. They had sworn to put aside prejudices and precon-ceptions and try the case solely on the evidence. They had been given a challenging and stressful task and consequently had spent 17 days weighing the evidence before making their decision. Now, however, it seemed the government was effectively overturning their considered verdicts.

It felt like a slap in the face, but despite their outrage, the jurors hesitated before doing anything. All had previously considered themselves apolitical; none had even so much as been on a protest march; accusing the British political establishment of foul play seemed like a big step. However, after talking it over, driven mainly by their concerns for the men's safety, they decided they couldn't stay silent.

After sounding out the other jurors, their first act was to email the editor of the *Guardian*, outlining their concerns. Within an hour, they had received a request for an interview. Two days later, three distinctly nervous jurors travelled to the *Guardian*'s offices in central London. (A fourth juror who supported their stance didn't feel able to take part in the interview for personal reasons.)

None of them had spoken to the press before; none had any idea what to expect. The result of the interview was a front-page article in the *Guardian* on 21 May, headlined: 'Jury Anger Over Threat of Torture'. It was an unprecedented piece which recounted the jurors' fury and frustration that the government was ignoring their verdict and acting as if the Algerians were guilty all along.

Although the *Guardian* article quoted them at length, the jurors remained anonymous for fear of a backlash. In the years since the case ended, although they have spoken extensively to different media, only the foreman, Lawrence Archer (co-author of this book), has ever been named publicly. The other two have remained anonymous because of concerns about the impact on their families and jobs. One of them, a civil servant, was specifically warned off by his senior manager from speaking about the case (although he has since changed his job).

The *Guardian* article provoked plaudits and condemnation in equal measure. The jurors were quoted condemning the Home Office for having 'totally disregarded' their decisions.

The move to deport the men was 'an outrage' and 'a total infringement of human rights'. They accused the government of acting out of spite and of 'playing to the gallery'. They also expressed great concern over the men's safety if they were returned to Algeria. Shami Chakrabarti, director of the human rights organisation Liberty, was also quoted in the article praising the 'principled stance' of the ricin jurors, as a 'great vindication of the continuing importance of jury trial in this country'.[18]

Jurors speaking up in this way, particularly in support of an unpopular group – illegal immigrants accused of terrorist offences – was something entirely new, and the article provoked a considerable response.

The three were invited to take part in a BBC *Panorama* programme about new anti-terror legislation, which covered Sidali Feddag's part in the ricin trial in some depth. One of them gave some idea of how she had been changed by the case. 'Before the trial, I had a lot of faith in the authorities to be making the right decisions on my behalf ... I never really gave it much thought. Whereas having been through this trial I'm very sceptical now as to the real reason why this new legislation is being pushed through.'[19] They also took part in several other documentaries – each time they were filmed in a way so as not to be recognised.

Michael Mansfield QC praised the jurors in a newspaper article for having 'exceptionally and courageously spoken out about the way their verdict has been nullified'. He added ruefully that government discomfort at their criticism would make 'minions in the Home Office' more determined than ever to try to scrap jury trials.[20]

Apart from becoming somewhat unlikely pundits on anti-terror legislation, life for the jurors had largely returned to normal. Lawrence Archer went back to his job as a telecoms engineer, and the other two also got on with their lives. They continued to meet up with each other and to follow political developments in the UK and Algeria with more interest than they had done before the trial.

Meanwhile, the three Algerians remained on immigration bail (set at a nominal amount), as they waited for their deportation cases to be heard. All were cautiously optimistic about remaining in the UK, having been advised they had a good chance of winning their deportation cases. Mustapha Taleb, the only former defendant allowed to work, found a job in an internet café. The other three filled their days as best they could.

On Thursday 7 July 2005, three bombs exploded within 50 seconds of each other on three London Underground trains. An hour later, a fourth bomb ripped through a double-decker bus in Tavistock Square. The explosions killed 56 people, including the four suicide bombers; 700 people were injured, many seriously. Two weeks later, on 21 July, the London transport system was attacked again by suicide bombers, although this time the there were no casualties as the four bombs failed to go off.

The government's reaction to the attacks came swiftly. On 5 August, prime minister Tony Blair made his infamous remark that: 'The rules of the game are changing.' Blair proposed a raft of anti-terror laws, including holding terror suspects for up to 90 days without charge. It was a highly contentious move and Blair was later to suffer his first ever parliamentary defeat on the 90-day issue, when MPs from all parties voted strongly against the proposal. The government was subsequently forced to compromise and the Terrorism

Act of 2006 included a pre-charge detention period of a maximum of 28 days. In 2008, this was extended to 42 days.

In the aftermath of the July suicide attacks, Blair also spoke of his government's determination to get tough on foreign terror suspects. He outlined the steps being taken to get around legal restrictions preventing foreign nationals being deported to countries with poor human rights records, like Algeria, Syria and Libya. His government was seeking to negotiate Memorandums of Understanding with these countries – promises that deportees would be given a fair trial and not mistreated. (Algeria consistently refused to sign, saying there was no need as it didn't go in for torture.) Blair added that he was prepared to change whatever laws were necessary, including the Human Rights Act, to see the changes go through.

Like everyone else in the capital, Mouloud Sihali, David Khalef, Sidali Feddag and Mustapha Taleb were shaken by the 7/7 and 21/7 attacks. However, they were trying to get on with their lives, and the ensuing political debate all seemed rather remote. Sihali, Khalef and Feddag continued to report to the police station once or twice a week (as required under their bail conditions), while they waited for their deportation cases to be heard.

On 15 September, Taleb and Sihali's relative peace was to be shattered: each was woken in the early hours by the arrival of dozens of armed police, bursting through their front doors to arrest them as 'threats to national security'.

As the prime minister had said, the rules of the game had, indeed, changed.

9

Legacy

In the summer of 2005, Britain was left reeling from the suicide attacks of 7 and 21 July. On 22 July, the Brazilian electrician Jean Charles de Menezes was shot dead by police at Stockwell Tube station, after being mistaken for one of the 21 July bombers who had fled when their devices failed to explode.

With the public understandably jittery in the wake of the attacks, the government mounted a show of strength to try to calm fears and demonstrate the effectiveness of its anti-terror policies.

The July bombers had been British-born Muslims but the Home Secretary responded to the attacks by ordering the re-arrest of several foreign nationals. Among those rounded up were two of the four defendants previously cleared in the ricin trial.

Early on the morning of the 15 September 2005, Mouloud Sihali was asleep in bed when he was woken by the sound of shouting and hammering at the street door of his flat. Sihali assumed it was his noisy neighbours again, but got up to have a look. Before he had a chance to go downstairs, the door to his flat burst open and a stream of police officers stormed up the stairs, some armed and wearing body armour. Sihali, barely awake, was terrified. Fearing he would be shot, he held up his hands and screamed: 'I didn't do anything!'

Sihali, who is tall but slimly built, was wearing only a T-shirt and boxer shorts. Five officers forced him to the floor and restrained him with such force that it caused permanent damage to his knee (he still walks with a limp). He was then handcuffed, put in a police van and taken to jail.

Over in north London, Mustapha Taleb was having a similarly rude awakening. At 6 a.m., officers stormed into his building, kicking in all the doors, even those of other residents. Taleb was woken by a loud bang on his door and before he had time to get up, was jumped on by five or six officers. He was hauled up and then thrown to the floor, face down while two officers stood on his hands. Taleb was so terrified that he vomited.

Later the same day, Home Secretary Charles Clarke announced a new package of anti-terror proposals, including 90-day pre-charge detention for suspects. Clarke subsequently denied that the arrests and announcement had been orchestrated, but it seems a remarkable coincidence – particularly given that Sihali had been at the immigration offices the day before for a routine visit and could easily have been detained while he was there.

Taleb and Sihali are not the only suspects to have been arrested with apparently unnecessary force. 'Detainee G', an Algerian man accused of supporting terrorist organisations, was subjected to a similarly dramatic dawn arrest a month earlier. He says: 'I was re-arrested in August 2005 when more than 50 immigration, police and special officers came to my home at 6 a.m. Seven to 10 officers came inside the house while the rest waited in the street with four police vans. The police refused to let me phone my lawyer and also refused to tell me or my wife where they planned to take me. I don't understand why the police had to come at that time in the morning and why so many of them came. After all, I was already under 24-hour surveillance and house arrest. I was always strictly monitored.'[1]

Although Taleb and Sihali had been arrested, they were not charged with any offence. Instead, they were told they were considered a threat to national security and were subject to a deportation order. No explanation was given as to why, after being allowed to move around freely in the four months since their acquittal at the Old Bailey, they were now suddenly deemed dangerous.

The pair were in despair to find themselves back in Belmarsh, having so recently being released from two years in prison awaiting trial. They were held for four months until January 2006, when their lawyers negotiated their release under strict bail conditions.

On release, Taleb and Sihali had to wear a tag around their ankle, linking them electronically to a machine which monitored when they were at home. Every time they went out or came back, they had to phone a security monitoring company. Both were subjected to regular and random searches, when two or three immigration officers would arrive without warning and go through all their possessions. At one point, Taleb's home was being searched up to three times a week.

They were curfewed for up to 20 hours a day and not allowed to step outside their front doors during this time. During the four hours a day when they were allowed out, they had to stay within a strictly defined area of about a square mile. If they needed to go further afield, say, for a hospital appointment, they had to apply for permission in advance stating where they wanted to go and why. They were denied mobile phones and internet access and had to report daily to a police station. No one was allowed to visit them at home unless previously vetted and approved by the Home Office, which involved visitors being designated a 'known associate of terrorists' (or KAT).

The men were to be referred to in the media by letters of the alphabet rather than their own names, something that Mouloud Sihali felt was an attempt to dehumanise them in the eyes of the public. (Both Sihali [AA] and Taleb [Y], later waived their anonymity.)

Technically, the restrictions on them were imposed as conditions of their immigration bail, but they were so strict, they amounted to a control order in all but name. The new Draconian restrictions were absurd given that before they were arrested in September, both men had been free to move around as they wished. Both were living openly in local authority housing. Sihali's only bail conditions were to register at an immigration office twice a week and post bail of £1,000. He wasn't allowed to work (while his asylum claim was pending) but other than that, Sihali could do what he liked. Taleb (who had been granted asylum in 2000) was even more unrestricted and, as already mentioned, got himself a job in an internet café. Now, he wasn't even allowed to own a mobile phone, let alone use the internet. Overnight and with no explanation, the pair had gone from being of minimal interest to the authorities to needing to be closely monitored and stringently controlled.

Initially, while living under his strict bail conditions, Taleb was housed in a flat very close to the Finsbury Park Mosque. It was a tiny, cell-like flat, which was often full of marijuana smoke, wafting up from the tenant downstairs. On one occasion, Taleb discovered a prostitute having sex with a client on his stairs. He was allowed out of the flat for just four hours a day and was often followed by the security forces during this time.

On one occasion, he spotted a young couple tailing him in a local park. Taleb raced off and hid behind a tree and watched as they looked around in a state of panic, making desperate calls on their mobile phones. Taleb then calmly reappeared behind them, tapped them on the shoulder and walked off.

Meanwhile, the three ricin jurors who had spoken to the press were still trying to establish contact with the cleared defendants. Having read so many contradictory reports, they wanted to hear the defendants' side of the story and also to show support in their fight against deportation.

After months of getting nowhere, they finally had a breakthrough when Mustapha Taleb's lawyers invited the three to attend his deportation hearing in May 2006. The case was to be heard in a tribunal known as the Special Immigration Appeals Commission, or SIAC, which decides the fate of foreign terror suspects facing deportation to countries with poor human rights records.

SIAC is nothing like a conventional English court: there is no jury and the case is heard by three judges who are specially vetted to hear evidence from the secret services. Much of the evidence is heard in secret – even the defendant and his lawyers won't know what it is. Often, the defendant will not even know what he is accused of – making the job of the defence all but impossible. As Mustapha Taleb puts it: 'You are fighting ghosts.'[2]

During the closed sessions, the accused is represented by a government-appointed 'special advocate'. These advocates, who are specially vetted barristers, are not allowed to pass any information back to the defendant. Instead, the defendant and his lawyer must try to guess what the allegations might be and instruct the special advocate accordingly. The process is not only extremely prejudicial, but could lead to a defendant confessing to a crime he is not actually accused of.

SIAC hearings and their reliance on secret evidence have been hugely controversial since the outset. In December 2004, the leading immigration barrister Ian Macdonald QC had resigned as a special advocate, describing SIAC as 'an odious blot on our legal landscape' and claiming that since 9/11, it had degenerated into 'an internment court'.

Macdonald pointed out that no other country in Europe had followed Britain in derogating from Article 5 of the European Convention in order to be able to detain suspects indefinitely without trial. He told a subsequent television documentary that terror suspects are being detained on the basis of little more than gossip. 'The problem with intelligence assessments is that you can never tell if they're any good or not. ... I've been told by a policeman that, as far as he's concerned, the material that intelligence people have was guesswork. ... Everyone thinks that intelligence is based on evidence, when intelligence is based on assessments ... some of it is evidence, but some of it may not be and certainly it's possibly third, fourth or fifth hand material, the reliability of which you can't properly assess.'[3]

Two of the jurors took up Taleb's lawyer's invitation and went along to the hearing, albeit with some trepidation. Taleb had seemed so hard and unreadable during the Old Bailey trial that they were nervous at encountering him again. When they arrived in the courtroom, they were in for a shock. Given that Taleb was accused of being a threat to national security, they'd expected to find him in the dock, surrounded by security guards. Instead, as the pair took their seats, they realised Taleb was sitting directly in front of them. This was the closest they had ever been to him and it felt extremely uncomfortable, but to their great surprise, during the lunchtime break, Taleb turned around and smiled at them, saying: 'Thank you for saving my life.'

At the end of the hearing, having heard Taleb accused of the most serious offences, the two jurors were even more surprised to see him head off to the bus stop, accompanied only by one of his supporters, a tiny bird-like woman.

When Taleb addressed them directly at SIAC, it was the first time that any of the defendants had spoken directly to the former jurors and it was a revelation. Until that point, the jurors had been acting almost on instinct, out of some innate belief in an abstract notion of justice and fair play. In that moment, the defendants became human, just like them.

For SIAC to order a deportation, two criteria have to be met. The commission has to be convinced the accused is a threat to national security and that, if returned to his home country, he is not in danger of being tortured or mistreated.

Taleb was accused of being a UK leader of the DHDS, an Algerian terrorist organisation, something he has always vigorously denied. He was also alleged to have taken part in the bombing of a train in Algeria, in which over 40 members of the security forces were killed, again something he strongly denies. Taleb himself suspects the accusation stems from someone who was tortured in Algeria, and that it is a case of mistaken identity. (With the description 'Mustapha from Tlemcen' applying equally to any number of his fellow countrymen.)

Taleb lost his initial case in SIAC, but has made several appeals against deportation. His lawyers argue that he faces a death sentence in Algeria, passed in his absence, for his alleged part in the train bombing. The sentence was subsequently commuted to life in prison following a moratorium on capital punishment. However, Taleb's lawyers argued it wasn't safe for him to return as the moratorium was at the whim of the current head of state in Algeria, President Bouteflika, and could be revoked by a future leader.

In February 2006, there seemed to a ray of hope that Taleb might be able to return home safely, as Bouteflika announced a six-month amnesty for anti-government rebels. SIAC prosecutors suggested that Taleb would qualify and could, therefore, be deported. However on closer investigation of the terms of the amnesty by the defence, it was clear he was unlikely to qualify as crimes of international terrorism were excluded from its remit.

In a breathtaking about-turn by the SIAC judges, Taleb's bail was revoked in August 2006 and he was returned to jail. They argued that he would abscond, knowing that he was likely to be detained if returned to Algeria, despite the prosecution's continued insistence that he would be in no danger if returned. Taleb subsequently spent over two years in Long Lartin prison in Worcestershire, before being released again on strict bail conditions at the end of 2008. This time, he was obliged by SIAC to live in a small provincial town, despite his lawyers' arguing he should be returned to London. Taleb had been on antidepressants during the Old Bailey trial and his mental health deteriorated dramatically following his re-arrest: a prison psychiatrist in Long Lartin deemed him a severe suicide risk.

Depression is common among detainees, borne of desperation and helplessness at not knowing when, if ever, their situation will be resolved. Many become clinically depressed, some have attempted suicide, one has been admitted to Broadmoor hospital with severe mental health problems. 'Detainee G' described his experience of being held in a special unit in Belmarsh to a journalist with the *Big Issue*: 'We were kept a minimum of 22 hours in this cell and never saw the sky', recalled G, who wasn't allowed to see his wife or have any visitors for six months. 'Then when she was allowed to visit, there was a screen and we had to communicate by phone ... In Britain I have less rights than an animal.'[4]

In 2007, four Algerian detainees could stand detention no longer and chose to return to Algeria. As they declared: 'We are choosing the alternative of a quick death in Algeria to a slow death here.'[5] Despite assurances that they wouldn't face charges, when they returned to Algeria, two of the men, Rida Dendani and Benaissa Taleb (no relation to Mustapha), were held for twelve days by the DRS before being charged, tried and convicted of 'international terrorism' in an Algerian court. Dendani was sentenced to eight years' imprisonment, Benaissa Taleb to three. Among the other detained men choosing to return was Omar Djedid, the associate of Mohammed Meguerba's who had been central to the ricin arrests. Djedid, however, was not picked up by the DRS and was soon to disappear off the radar.

Shortly after meeting Mustapha Taleb for the first time in May 2006, the jurors managed to make contact with two other cleared defendants, David Khalef and Mouloud Sihali. Sihali was under strict immigration bail conditions at the time, so the jurors met him for lunch in Sihali's vetted area. Khalef arrived first and met them at the Tube station, all boyish grins and kisses on the cheek. Sihali arrived later, limping noticeably from his knee injury. Khalef was amiable but quiet and obviously struggled to read the lunch menu, although he was taking a literacy course to improve his English. Sihali seemed uncomfortable that he could not afford to entertain his guests in traditional Algerian style. He ordered the cheapest item on the menu when the jurors insisted on paying. At the time, he was surviving on a government handout of £40 a week.

That encounter was awkward and stilted at first but Sihali was soon in full flow. He was desperate to tell the jurors as much as possible about his life and the lead up to the trial. The former foreman rapidly filled dozens of pages of a notebook with information, dates and names concerning the ricin conspiracy. Inevitably, they spoke about the trial and the jurors were amused by the two men's thoughts on the jury. One juror who sometimes scowled, although only with back pain, was assumed by the defendants to be a real 'hanger and flogger'; another who fancied himself as a ladies' man was assumed by the defendants to be gay.

Sihali was still under strict curfew so, with much still left to discuss, the group had to break up. As they walked towards Sihali's flat, the foreman asked how he saw the future if his asylum claim were successful. Sihali's reply was caustic: he felt his life had been irreparably blighted by the ricin allegations. He saw no future in the UK (or anywhere in Europe), as he would be constantly picked up by the anti-terror police, whenever they were rounding up the 'usual suspects'. He would never get a proper job, as he would have to explain long absences from employment to any prospective employer. His only hope, he thought, was to clear his name through SIAC.

Before the group headed their separate ways, they stopped to take a photo to mark what had been a significant occasion for all of them. The photo shows Khalef with his arm around one juror's shoulders and both of them grinning at the camera; Sihali stands apart with downcast eyes and a sorrowful expression. After the photo was taken, Sihali wandered off disconsolately to get back to his flat in time for the curfew.

Khalef walked with the jurors to the tube station, chatting away as if they were old friends, before setting off back home. As he departed, he kissed the former foreman three times on the cheek, 'because this is what you do in my country if you are a special friend'. The foreman was flattered and embarrassed in equal amounts.

The four defendants had stood alongside each other in the dock during the ricin trial. They had been acquitted and released together but after that their fates had diverged. David Khalef and Sidali Feddag were not picked up in the raids of September 2005, which saw Sihali and Taleb returned to prison and then put on highly restrictive bail conditions.

After his acquittal, Khalef was housed by the immigration authorities, first in west London, and then in Manchester. At his asylum hearing in August 2008, the government case against him was half-hearted and confused. The prosecution stated that in Meguerba's confessions to the DRS (which had sparked the ricin arrests), he mentioned two associates called 'Djamal' – which was one of the aliases Khalef used regularly. Perhaps, the prosecution now suggested, Khalef was not the Djamal that Meguerba had been referring to as one of the ricin plotters; if so, Khalef was under no threat if he were to be returned to Algeria. This line of argument drew an incredulous response from the judge: was the prosecutor saying the wrong man had been taken to court?

In October 2008, Khalef was granted the right to stay in the UK for five years, a term which will be extended if he stays out of trouble. He is allowed to work (although is currently unemployed) and can travel abroad freely. He now lives quietly in London.

The fourth ricin defendant, the teenager Sidali Feddag, was initially taken under the wing of his trial solicitor, Julian Hayes, before being 'adopted' and taken in by a family in Kent. Unlike Mouloud Sihali whose experiences left him disillusioned with British justice, Feddag was left deeply impressed by the jury system. He became interested in legal affairs and began to do unpaid work at Julian Hayes' firm. In 2006, he did an access course before going on to start a law degree in 2007. Unable to do paid work until comparatively recently (due to his immigration status), Feddag has been forced to rely on the generosity of others who have funded his studies.

Of all the ricin defendants, Feddag is probably the one who has most successfully rebuilt his life. The skinny, spotty youth who sat hunched in the Old Bailey dock is now a muscular, well-groomed and confident young man who loves Britain and wants to be a lawyer. He lives with his British-born Algerian wife in London and is working part-time in a pizza restaurant while he studies. He is still awaiting the outcome of his asylum claim.

Mouloud Sihali's spirits had been crushed by his re-arrest, especially as the evidence against him in the Secretary of State's deportation case was just a rehash of the allegations from the ricin trial. Worse, he had no idea how long he would be in legal limbo as his lawyers sought to fight his deportation.

The support from the Algerian community in north London which had previously sustained him had long since fallen away, for fear that associating with a suspected terrorist would bring trouble to their doors.

Aside from a handful of people from charity organisations, Sihali had few visitors during his 20 hours of curfew. In summer 2006, two of the ricin jurors overcame their misgivings about being labelled KATs ('known associates of terrorists') to get Home Office clearance to visit Sihali at home (the third juror decided against, for fear of damaging his career). Over subsequent months, the two jurors became regular visitors, striking up a very real, if unlikely, friendship with the former defendant, which continues to this day.

To Sihali, his life seemed even worse than when he was in prison and he descended into depression and paranoia. The stress he was under not only damaged his mental health but also caused physical problems. He began to suffer blurred eyesight, along with chest pains and shortness of breath. Initially, his condition was dismissed as asthma, before a local GP who took a particular interest in his case diagnosed him correctly as suffering from sarcoidosis. Sarcoidosis is a rare but potentially fatal lung disease, which can also affect the eyes. Sihali was diagnosed as suffering depression and post-traumatic shock, involving flashbacks of the armed police storming into his flat, and his GP subsequently complained that Sihali's 'brutal' bail conditions were preventing his patient getting proper treatment for his condition. At one point, Sihali cut short an appointment at Moorfields Eye Hospital as he was terrified of being out for longer than the extra hour-and-a-half agreed to by the Home Office. 'Without a shadow of a doubt, the accommodation and other restrictions he's under pose a serious risk to his mental and physical health and have resulted in delayed treatment', said his doctor.[6]

In the summer of 2006, Sihali's medical treatment was further disrupted when the immigration authorities moved him from Hoxton in east London, to a small house in Colnbrook, close to Heathrow airport. His status as a supposed threat to national security was unchanged but when he first moved, there were no restrictions imposed on his movements. For the first six weeks, Sihali was free to go wherever he wanted during his allotted hours (which by now had been extended to six hours a day) and he travelled up to London several times. When the authorities finally got around to specifying where he could and couldn't go, perhaps surprisingly given he was accused of plotting to use poisons and explosives, his allocated area incorporated Heathrow Airport, a company which supplied food to the airlines, two major motorways and a huge reservoir.

Later that year, Sihali was moved back to London, where he remains to this day. He has a tiny room which is the exact dimensions of his former prison cell. His mental health remains fragile. At one point, he covered the smoke detector in his room with tinfoil as he was paranoid it was concealing a camera or microphone. He would get very agitated when the entry phone sounded, as he associated the buzzer with the unannounced arrival of immigration officers to search his property, so regular visitors got in the habit of tapping on his window when they arrived.

In 2006, Sihali renounced his anonymity and, in an unexpected development, went on to become the 'poster boy' of the Algerian detainees. Tall, handsome and articulate, he was an ideal interviewee and has appeared in numerous radio and TV programmes. His case featured heavily in the Channel 4 *Dispatches* documentary, 'At Home With the Terror Suspects' and the cinema release *Taking Liberties*. Sihali even featured in a lengthy and flattering article in the US glossy magazine *Vanity Fair*,[7] when the American political reporter William Langewiesche and a fashion photographer were flown to the UK specially for the assignment. The ensuing 21-page piece ran alongside articles about the likes of Harrison Ford and Princess Diana, and included full-page photos of Sihali dressed in a fashionable dark coloured jacket and cashmere scarf bought for him by the magazine.

There have been no glossy magazine photo shoots for the less photogenic Mustapha Taleb. Since his re-arrest in 2005, he has never been charged with any offence or even interviewed by police. At the time of writing, he waits for his case to go to the Court of Appeal. If this appeal fails, the European Court of Human Rights in Strasbourg is the last legal avenue open to him to prevent deportation. Even then, he is likely to remain in legal limbo for several years as the European court has a huge backlog of cases. In the meantime, Taleb vegetates in his tiny house, kept barely sane by a regime of prescription drugs and occasional visits from a handful of approved visitors. He revels in hearing the mundane stuff of everyday family life, something that he believes he can never have. He was briefly engaged, but called it off, fearing that his bad luck would rub off on his fiancée. His father died in 2009, but Taleb could not attend the funeral in Algeria or comfort his elderly mother, who is virtually blind with cataracts. When asked about his hopes for the future, he recalled his grandfather who had been a hothead when he was younger. As he grew older, the grandfather had settled on a farm in the mountains with a few chickens and goats. Taleb and his brother had ridiculed the old man for losing the fire in his belly, but now Taleb envied the old man's lifestyle and would have gladly settled for it himself.

When Mouloud Sihali's deportation case eventually went to SIAC in March 2007, Michael Mansfield QC represented him as defence barrister once again. The government's case was based almost entirely on his alleged involvement in the ricin conspiracy, his fraudulent use of false identity documents and his connections with Mohammed Meguerba, despite Sihali's having been acquitted of these charges at trial. Mansfield repeated his cross-examination demolition of a prosecution witness: this time, Mansfield's victim was a government official known as Witness A. She testified that Sihali had been convicted at the ricin trial of possessing the fake passports that had been found in the base of the bed at Ilford, when, in fact, he had been cleared of these charges. (He had previously pleaded guilty to having the false passports in the names Omar Nait Atmane and Cristophe Riberro.) Mansfield tore into Witness A, asking where she had got her information and she admitted she had simply typed Sihali's name into Google. The admission caused uproar in the court.

Two months later, in May 2007, SIAC judges cleared Sihali of being a threat to national security, and he was immediately taken off his strict bail conditions. Mr Justice Mitting, chairing the commission, ruled there was no 'evidence or intelligence that he has ever been a principled Islamist extremist'. The judges were satisfied that although 'unprincipled', Sihali had not engaged in anything beyond petty dishonesty. 'Whatever the risk to national security he may have posed in 2002, the risk now is insignificant', they concluded.[8]

Sihali was still not out of the woods. Although no longer deemed a danger to national security, the decision about whether to grant him asylum was referred back to the Home Office. After considering the case for nearly two years, in 2009 the Home Office decided to refer the decision about his fate back to SIAC. After multiple postponements, his appeal was heard and rejected by the commission in March 2010. He is hoping to mount a further appeal against deportation back to Algeria.

In the meantime, Sihali still lives in his cell of a room in north London, surviving on £40 a week. His health has stabilised since his bail conditions have eased. He dreams of being able to start afresh, marry and raise a family, with no 'terrorist' label around his neck.

Mohammed Meguerba, the man who although physically absent from the ricin trial was so central to the case, was reportedly held in secret detention in Algeria for 17 months after his arrest in December 2002. He was subsequently moved to Sakardji prison in Algeria.[9] Unconfirmed reports suggest he was finally tried in his home country and received a 10-year prison sentence for crimes not related to the ricin plot.

The Finsbury Park Mosque, which had been the common thread linking all the defendants, was reopened for worship in October 2004. Keen to shrug off its reputation as a hotbed of radicalism, it has subsequently rebranded itself as the North London Central Mosque, boasting 'a new board of trustees with a new management team, new Imams, a new name and a new ethos'.[10]

And what of the fifth man, Kamel Bourgass, the only defendant actually convicted in relation to the ricin plot?

Since the Old Bailey trial, Bourgass has appealed separately against his convictions for the murder of DC Oake and the conspiracy to cause a public nuisance at the ricin case. Both appeals were rejected and he remains in a high-security prison.

Despite his incarceration, Bourgass continues to make headlines. In January 2009, there were press reports that he was demanding female prison officers wear veils and was trying to radicalise other prisoners. 'In one incident Bourgass, 33, outraged staff by sneering that the metal used for DC Stephen Oake's posthumous Queen's Gallantry Medal "came from my knife".' He was described as 'very abusive and confrontational', claiming that female officers in prayer meetings are 'a breach of his human rights'.[11] He has reportedly been attacked in prison and his cell set on fire by other prisoners.

Bourgass is currently serving consecutive sentences of 22 years for murder and 17 years for conspiracy. With his appeals having failed, he is unlikely to be released any time much before 2040. Once he has served his sentence, he will almost certainly face deportation – provided of course the authorities can establish what country this man, about whom so little is still known, actually comes from.

Appendices

A. DRAMATIS PERSONAE

The Algerians

Kamel Bourgass (aliases include: Nadir Habra; Omar Rami; Hans; El Moutaez)
Chief conspirator in the ricin plot and writer of the poison recipes. Alleged to have manufactured toxins in Wood Green. Fled to Manchester when news broke of the police raid on Wood Green. Murdered DC Stephen Oake and wounded three other officers when he was eventually arrested in Manchester. Convicted in two separate trials for murder and (in the ricin trial) of conspiracy to cause a public nuisance. Currently serving consecutive jail sentences of 22 and 17 years. At different times, Bourgass has given various different accounts of his life and background. Little is known about him definitively, but it is thought he was born in 1973 and entered the UK illegally in 2000.

Omar Djedid (aka: Detainee K)
Arrested in an internet café alongside Mouloud Sihali but never charged in connection with ricin plot. Had previously escaped from immigration detention in February 2002. Subsequently worked in markets with Mohammed Meguerba, and shared a room with Mouloud Sihali and David Khalef. Born in 1974, entered UK in 1998. After being held in detention, voluntarily agreed to be deported to Algeria in 2007.

Sidali Feddag
The youngest of the trial defendants, just 17 at the time of his arrest. Born in 1985, he entered the UK with his father in 2000 and claimed asylum. Given local authority housing in Wood Green as he waited for result of his asylum claim. Allowed acquaintance Kamel Bourgass to stay at the Wood Green flat, which was subsequently raided by anti-terror

police; poison-making and other suspect equipment discovered. Cleared in the ricin trial. Now married to a UK-born Algerian woman and studying law. Still awaiting a decision on his asylum claim.

David Aissa Khalef (aliases include: Djamel)
Alleged by the prosecution to have provided safekeeping for one of the poison recipes, but cleared of all charges by the jury. Low IQ and largely illiterate, with poor understanding of English. Born 1972 and entered the UK illegally in 1999. Shared a room with Mouloud Sihali in Ilford. Pleaded guilty to possession of false passports found at Ilford. Granted asylum in the UK in 2008, permitted to work and travel outside UK.

Mohammed Meguerba (aliases include: Sofiane; Bruno Charles Meurillon)
Co-conspirator in the ricin plot (along with Kamel Bourgass) but never charged in the UK, as he had fled to Algeria in 2002. His confessions to the Algerian secret service (almost certainly obtained under torture) were the catalyst for the arrests which led to the ricin trial. Owner of Seven Roses confectionary company. Friend of Omar Djedid. Lived in Ireland from 1995. Born in 1968, he came to London legally in 2002. Shared accommodation with Mouloud Sihali. Arrested and questioned by British police in September 2002, but subsequently released. Fled to Algeria, where he was captured and interrogated. Tried and jailed in 2005 and believed to be serving a 10-year sentence in Algeria on charges unrelated to the ricin plot.

Mouloud Sihali (aliases include: Omar Nait Atmane; Cristophe Riberro)
Alleged by the prosecution to be the plot's 'Mr Fix-it' but cleared by the jury of all charges. Born in 1976, entered the UK illegally in 1997. Shared a room with David Khalef. Provided accommodation in Ilford for Mohammed Meguerba and Omar Djedid. Company secretary of Mohammed Meguerba's business, Seven Roses. Gave information to police on the whereabouts of David Khalef, which led to the discovery of poison recipes in Thetford, Norfolk. Although cleared at the Old Bailey, was re-arrested in September 2005 as a 'threat to national security' and detained before being bailed under control-order conditions. Cleared of all suspicion of being a threat to national security by SIAC in May

2007. Still facing threat of deportation to Algeria following rejection of asylum appeal by SIAC in March 2010. Further appeal planned.

Mustapha Taleb (aka: Detainee Y)
Accused by prosecution of photocopying the poison recipe found at David Khalef's room in Norfolk, using the copier at Finsbury Park Mosque. Cleared of all charges by the jury. Born in 1969 and entered the UK in 2000. Won political asylum in 2000 after providing evidence of having been tortured in Algeria. Worked at Finsbury Park Mosque bookshop during 2002. After acquittal, re-arrested (along with Mouloud Sihali) in September 2005 as a 'threat to national security'. Since then, has been variously imprisoned in Long Lartin or held under control-order conditions.

The Lawyers

Ben Emerson QC
Defence barrister for Mustapha Taleb.

Julian Hayes
Criminal defence solicitor; represented teenage defendant Sidali Feddag.

Toby Hedworth QC
Defence barrister for Sidali Feddag.

Michael Mansfield QC
Defence barrister for Mouloud Sihali.

Michel Massih QC
Defence barrister for Kamel Bourgass.

Gareth Peirce
Leading human rights and criminal defence solicitor; represented Mouloud Sihali, David Khalef and Mustapha Taleb.

David Penry-Davey
The Honourable Mr Justice Penry-Davey; judge at the ricin trial, held at the Old Bailey.

Marguerite Russell
Defence barrister for David Khalef.

Nigel Sweeney QC
Prosecution barrister at the ricin trial.

Old Bailey witnesses

Dr A
Senior scientist at the UK government's Porton Down science facility; tested items found at Wood Green flat for evidence of poisons.

Andrew Gould
Porton Down manager who gave evidence at the ricin trial, with responsibility for passing on test results to police.

The Politicians

Tony Blair MP
Prime Minister of Britain May 1997–May 2007.

David Blunkett MP
Home Secretary, June 2001–December 2004.

Charles Clarke MP
Home Secretary, December 2004–May 2006.

Colin Powell
United States Secretary of State, January 2001–January 2005.

The Police

Sir Ian Blair
Chief Constable, Metropolitan Police Service, 2005–2008.

DC Stephen Oake
Detective Constable with the Manchester police force. Stabbed to death by Kamel Bourgass.

B. TIMELINE

1992
A military coup in Algeria prompts a bloody civil war, where civilians bear much of the brunt of the violence. As the economy collapses and chaos spreads, those who are able to flee leave Algeria for Europe.

1997
Mouloud Sihali arrives illegally in the UK from Algeria.

1998
David Khalef arrives illegally in the UK.

2000
Mustapha Taleb arrives illegally in the UK. He is later granted asylum, after providing evidence of torture.

Sidali Feddag arrives in the UK. Feddag fails to attend immigration hearings and overstays illegally.

Kamel Bourgass arrives illegally in the UK. He applies for political asylum and is given housing in Manchester while he waits for his case to be heard.

Mohammed Meguerba becomes converted to radical Islam in Ireland.

2001
Omar Djedid arrested, but later escapes from immigration detention.

Meguerba allegedly trains at Afghan terror camp with Kamel Bourgass.

11 September: Al-Qaeda attacks on the World Trade Centre and the Pentagon.

November: Anti-terrorism, Crime and Security Act 2001 introduced, allowing for the indefinite detention of terror suspects without charge.

Seventeen men are held under this new ruling, commonly known as 'Belmarsh Powers'.

December: Kamel Bourgass's asylum appeal rejected. He disappears off the radar and continues living illegally in the UK (probably sleeping at the Finsbury Park Mosque).

2002
Operation Springbourne is launched by British anti-terror police to investigate terrorist funding.

March: Mohammed Meguerba arrives in the UK. He meets up with Omar Djedid and the pair start selling sweets in markets.

Spring: David Khalef goes to work in Norfolk, leaving Mouloud Sihali to look after his room at 240 High Road, Ilford. Sihali takes on a false identity (Cristophe Riberro) and starts renting his own property, 103d Elgin Road, Ilford. Sidali Feddag allows Bourgass to stay in his room in Wood Green.

Summer: Bourgass meets Meguerba and they begin plotting. David Khalef allows Omar Djedid and Meguerba to stay in his room. Sihali later agrees they can use his flat at Elgin Road.

July: Sihali becomes company secretary of Meguerba's business, Seven Roses.

August: Sihali throws Meguerba out of the Elgin Road flat.

18 September: Meguerba is picked up by police, and released on bail. Police find Sihali's Elgin Road address in his wallet. Meguerba flees and ends up in Algeria.

19 September: Police put Elgin Road under surveillance and spot Omar Djedid, who is arrested, along with Mouloud Sihali. Sihali leads them to Khalef's room at 240 High Road. Police find Meguerba's passport and other papers at Sihali's flat.

26 September: Police trace Khalef to his Norfolk address and find a photocopy of the poison recipes in his bag.

December: Bourgass moves out of Feddag's Wood Green flat and stays at Finsbury Park Mosque.

16 December: Meguerba picked up and interrogated by Algerian police. He confesses to the poison plot.

2003

5 January: Anti-terror police raid the Wood Green address. Suspect items tested for ricin and show an initial 'weak positive'. Further poison recipes and other incriminating evidence found. Feddag arrested.

7 January: Further testing by scientists at Porton Down rules out presence of ricin. Porton Down manager Andrew Gould tells police the opposite: that ricin has been found. UK Health Secretary and Home Secretary issue a joint public statement about the find. The NHS issues advice that the public should not panic. Finsbury Park Mosque bookshop worker Mustapha Taleb is arrested.

8 January: News of 'ricin factory' breaks in media. Kamel Bourgass flees to Manchester.

14 January: Police attempt to arrest Bourgass. Bourgass kills DC Stephen Oake and wounds three other officers.

20 January: Finsbury Park Mosque raided in Operation Mermant. Weapons and false papers seized.

22 January: Eight people arrested in connection with developing a chemical weapon.

5 February: Colin Powell tells UN Security Council ricin was discovered in London and links it to Al-Qaeda and Iraq. The ricin plot is cited as a reason to go to war with Iraq.

20 March: US and UK forces attack Iraq. Porton Down finally tells the government that no ricin was found at Wood Green.

31 March: General Richard Myers, US Commander in Chief, claims a site found in Iraq is where operatives were trained to make poisons: 'We think that's probably where the ricin found in London came from.' No poisons were ever found at the site.

October: UK police interview Meguerba in Algeria.

2004
June: Bourgass is convicted of murdering DC Oake and sentenced to 22 years. Press blackout on the case to avoid prejudicing ricin trial.

August: Finsbury Park Mosque preacher Abu Hamza is arrested.

September: Ricin trial begins at Old Bailey. Defendants are Mouloud Sihali, David Khalef, Mustapha Taleb, Sidali Feddag and Kamel Bourgass.

December: House of Lords quashes Belmarsh Powers on human rights grounds.

2005
11 March: 'Control orders' introduced to replace Belmarsh Powers (Prevention of Terrorism Act 2005). Some 60 Labour MPs rebel and vote against, cutting the government's majority to 14. The men previously held in Belmarsh are immediately put on control orders.

8 April: In the ricin trial at the Old Bailey, Bourgass is convicted of conspiracy to cause a public nuisance; the four other defendants acquitted of all charges. Jury discharged after failing to reach a verdict on Bourgass's second charge, conspiracy to murder. Bourgass sentenced to 17 years' imprisonment for the nuisance charge. A follow-on trial of four other 'ricin' defendants and a retrial of Bourgass on conspiracy to murder charges is subsequently abandoned.

17 April: Sir Ian Blair, then Met police chief, says new anti-terror laws are needed in the wake of the ricin acquittals.

May: UK government announces its intention to deport the four acquitted men to Algeria. Article appears in the *Guardian* ('Jury anger over threat of torture').

7 July: Terrorist bomb attacks kill 56 people on the London transport system.

21 July: Second attack on London transport system – although this time the bombs fail to explode.

22 July: Jean Charles de Menezes is shot dead by police firearms officers at Stockwell Tube station.

5 August: Tony Blair announces the introduction of new security measures, including tougher powers of deportation. 'The rules of the game are changing', he says.

15 September: Sihali and Taleb arrested as 'threats to national security'.

9 November: In the House of Commons, Home Secretary Charles Clarke announces proposals for 90-day detention without charge. Proposals are defeated by parliament.

2006
January: Sihali and Taleb released from Belmarsh Prison and put on control-order style regimes.

March: Terrorism Act 2006 becomes law, including provision for 28-day detention without trial.

May: Three former ricin jurors meet Sihali, Khalef and Taleb for first time.

August: Mustapha Taleb sent to Long Lartin prison; his appeal against deportation is denied.

2007
14 May: Mouloud Sihali wins his appeal in SIAC and is released from control-order conditions.

2008
June: 42-day pre-charge detention of terror suspects is approved by the House of Commons.

October: Khalef wins right to stay in the UK. Mustapha Taleb is released from prison under control-order conditions.

2009
Taleb's deportation case is referred to the Court of Appeal.

Sidali Feddag starts his final year of a law degree course.

2010
March: Mouloud Sihali's asylum appeal rejected by SIAC.

C. SIGNIFICANT ADDRESSES

240 High Road, Ilford, Essex

David Khalef lived in a top-floor room at this address. Accommodation was provided for him at the end of 1998 while his asylum claim was being processed. The property is above shops and divided into five bed-sits, with shared kitchen and bathroom. Mouloud Sihali was the first to move in with Khalef, but the room was subsequently also used by Mohammed Meguerba and Omar Djedid, particularly when Khalef moved to Norfolk (see below) for work.

Items found at 240

Property searched by police in September 2002, after they arrested Sihali and Djedid at an internet café. Items recovered included two false passports belonging to Sihali (in names of Omar Atmane and Cristophe Riberro) and his genuine Algerian ID card. Also recovered were several stolen or doctored passports, found in the bed base. One of the altered passports was in the name of Dahlab, but bore a picture of Rabah Kadre, who Mohammed Meguerba claimed was number two in the European Al-Qaeda network. Khalef claimed he was looking after them for an (un-named) acquaintance.

103d Elgin Road, Ilford, Essex

Flat rented by Mouloud Sihali in summer 2002. Property is about a 20-minute walk from 240 High Road. Sihali later allowed Mohammed Meguerba and Omar Djedid to stay there.

Items found at 103

Meguerba's locked computer bag contained a diary and false passport in name of Bruno Charles Meurillon (the name he had used to set up Seven Roses). The diary had a phone number in Pakistan, crudely encoded into a series of distances shown on a map. There were printed business cards for Seven Roses in the living room. Also recovered was a print-out of an internet article containing a speech by Osama bin Laden, thought to belong to Omar Djedid.

352b High Road, Wood Green, London

The 15-year-old Sidali Feddag was given this one-bedroom flat above a pharmacy in September 2001, while he waited for his asylum claim to be heard. Feddag let Kamel Bourgass stay in his room, but asked the latter to move out shortly before Christmas 2002, so that Feddag's brother, Samir, could move in. Only Samir Feddag was there when the police raided.

Items found at 352b

Most of the suspect items that featured in the ricin trial were found at 352b. Bourgass had left most of his belongings behind at Feddag's flat when he fled to Manchester. In a locked sports bag (with the key in the outside pocket), police discovered the original full-sized version of the poison recipes, plus a smaller, folded-up version, and £4,100 in cash.

A photocopied version of the recipes was stuffed into the bottom drawer of the wardrobe. Another drawer contained foil sweet wrappers belonging to Bourgass (which he used in his shoplifting activities). A Nivea face-cream jar, containing an attempt at making nicotine poison, was found in a compartment inside the wardrobe.

In the bottom wardrobe compartment there were jars containing herbs and honey, plus, hidden at the back, two bottles of acetone and one of isopropanol. On top of the wardrobe was a set of kitchen scales and a small quantity of cherry stones wrapped in paper were in the scales pan. Down the side of the wardrobe was a disposable cup containing a small quantity of apple seeds. A small quantity of castor beans (the raw ingredient for ricin poison) was found in a chest of drawers.

Police also found various pairs of domestic rubber gloves, latex surgical gloves, funnels, blotting paper and several thermometers, plus a set of electronic scales for accurately measuring small weights. There was a handwritten calculation on the scales' instruction sheet which directly correlated to the proportions for making ricin in the recipes.

Police also found a marble pestle and mortar and a stainless steel coffee mill, allegedly used for grinding up poison ingredients (although it ultimately tested negative for traces of ricin). Another sports bag contained various unopened bottles of toiletries and several toothbrushes. The prosecution suggested that Bourgass intended to put poisons into the products or on to the toothbrush bristles and then put them back into shops. Bourgass said he intended sending them home to his family.

Finsbury Park Mosque, 7–11 St Thomas Road, London

Opened in 1994, the mosque became the centre of 'Little Algiers', a meeting point for the immigrant Algerian population in London. As well as a place of worship, the mosque served an unofficial purpose as a social centre, canteen, shop and advice centre. The notorious firebrand preacher Abu Hamza has become indelibly associated with the mosque. Hamza was eventually arrested and sentenced to seven years' imprisonment in early 2006, convicted of inciting murder and race hatred and one count of a terrorist offence.

Items found at mosque

The mosque was raided by the police in January 2003 following the discovery of its address on an envelope in Feddag's flat. The raid on the mosque unearthed a large quantity of false IDs, chequebooks and credit cards as well as a small cache of 'military equipment'. Subsequently the mosque remained closed until October 2004.

9 Ethel Coleman Way, Thetford, Norfolk

David Khalef was living at this address in September 2002 when he was arrested. It is a small house on a modern housing estate. Khalef shared a twin room with a Portuguese man and worked as unskilled labour in several chicken and pork factories in the area.

Items found at Thetford

A search of Khalef's room revealed a photocopy of the original handwritten poison recipes tucked into his suitcase, together with a false passport and driving licence.

4 Crumpsall Lane, Crumpsall, Manchester

Kamel Bourgass fled to Crumpsall Lane after hearing of the raid on Wood Green. It is a small one-bed flat in a converted Victorian house. Police raided the address on 14 January 2003 to arrest another man, unaware that Bourgass had been holed-up there for several days. He was arrested and, as he attempted to escape, murdered DC Stephen

Oake and injured three other officers. A torn-up passport belonging to Mohammed Meguerba was found in a rubbish bag at the Crumpsall Lane address, which suggests that he probably passed through the flat on his way to Algeria.

Notes

Chapter 1: The Trial

1. *Sun*, 9 January 2003.
2. *Daily Mail*, 13 January 2003.
3. BBC News website, 8 January 2003.
4. BBC News website, 10 January 2003.
5. *Independent*, 12 January 2003.
6. *Independent*, 14 February 1996.
7. *Sun*, 8 January 2003.
8. *Daily Mirror*, 8 January 2003.
9. SIAC appeal ruling notes SC/36/2003. Y and the Secretary for the Home Department, 24 August 2006.

Chapter 2: The Road From Algeria to the UK

1. Interview with Lawrence Archer.
2. Interview with Lawrence Archer.

Chapter 3: Everything Changes on 9/11

1. Interview with Lawrence Archer.
2. Wesley Gryk, former Law Society council member for immigration, senior partner at Wesley Gryk Solicitors, London.
3. Interview with Lawrence Archer.
4. Sean O'Neill and Daniel McGrory, *The Suicide Factory: Abu Hamza and the Finsbury Park Mosque*, Harper Collins, 2006.
5. Ibid.
6. *Sun* Editorial, 'Freeloaders', 13 September 2003.
7. *Daily Mail*, 10 January 2003.

8. Colin Powell, US Secretary of State, Address to the United Nations Security Council, 5 February 2003.

Chapter 4: Mohammed Meguerba

1. *Sunday Mirror*, 24 April 2005.
2. Amnesty International Report: 'United Kingdom. Deportation of Terror Suspects', EUR 45/046/2005, 20 October 2005.
3. *The Times*, 9 May 2005.

Chapter 5: Arrests

1. Interview with Lawrence Archer.
2. Interview with Lawrence Archer.
3. *Sunday Times*, 17 November 2002.
4. *Independent on Sunday*, 17 November 2001.
5. BBC News, 7 January 2003.
6. Sir John Stevens, *Not For the Fainthearted: My Life Fighting Crime*, Weidenfeld & Nicolson, 2005.

Chapter 6: Kamel Bourgass

1. *Daily Mirror*, 8 January 2003.
2. *Sun*, 8 January 2003.
3. *Daily Mail*, 10 January 2003.
4. BBC News, 16 February 2006.

Chapter 7: What Ricin?

1. Colin Powell, United States Secretary of State, Address to the United Nations Security Council, 5 February 2003.
2. *Independent*, 7 January 2003.
3. BBC News, 7 January 2003.
4. Sir Ian Blair, *Policing Controversy*, Profile Books, 2009.
5. *Independent*, 16 September 2005.

6. Val McDermid, *Beneath the Bleeding*, Harper Collins, 2007.
7. *Bad Girls*, Shed Productions, Series 8, Episode 1, 2006.
8. *Independent on Sunday*, 17 April 2005.
9. *Sun*, 8 January 2003.

Chapter 8: Backlash

1. *Daily Mail*, 14 April 2005.
2. *Daily Express*, 14 April 2005.
3. *Daily Mirror*, 14 April 2005.
4. *Sun*, 14 April 2005.
5. BBC, *Breakfast with Frost*, 17 April 2005.
6. *Guardian*, 14 April 2005.
7. Ibid.
8. Ibid. Note: the original article was withdrawn from the *Guardian* website as Campbell had directly named the Porton Down scientist designated 'Dr A', whose identity was concealed during the trial because of concerns about attacks from animal rights extremists (Porton Down conducts experiments on animals). A revised version has since been substituted.
9. BBC News, 8 January 2003.
10. BBC, *The Politics Show*, 14 November 2002.
11. BBC Radio 4, *Today*, 20 November 2002.
12. BBC News, 18 November 2002.
13. BBC News, 14 April 2005.
14. *Guardian*, 16 April 2005.
15. Michael Mansfield, *Memoirs of a Radical Lawyer*, Bloomsbury Press, 2009.
16. Select Committee on Home Affairs fourth report, Appendix: Police briefing note, 5 October 2005.
17. *Guardian*, 14 May 2005.
18. *Guardian*, 21 May 2005.
19. BBC, *Panorama*, 'Blair vs Blair', 9 October 2005.
20. *Independent*, 6 November 2005.

Chapter 9: Legacy

1. *Independent*, 15 December 2005.
2. Interview with Lawrence Archer.
3. Channel 4, *Dispatches*, 'At Home With the Terror Suspects', 5 February 2007.
4. Paul Donovan, 'State Britain', *Big Issue*, 19 March 2007.
5. Paul Donovan, 'Out of Control Orders', *New Statesman*, 17 April 2008.
6. Fiona Bawdon, 'Unhealthy Punishment', *New Statesman*, 15 January 2007.
7. William Langewiesche, 'A Face in the Crowd', *Vanity Fair*, February 2008.
8. *Guardian*, 15 May 2007.
9. *The Times*, 9 May 2005.
10. North London Central Mosque website.
11. *Daily Mirror*, 27 January 2009.

Index

Compiled by Sue Carlton

Page numbers in **bold** refer to photograph captions